Migrant Education
A REFERENCE HANDBOOK

Other Titles in
ABC-CLIO's
CONTEMPORARY EDUCATION ISSUES
Series

African American Education, Cynthia L. Jackson
Charter Schools, Danny Weil
School Vouchers and Privatization, Danny Weil
Special Education, Arlene Sacks
Student Rights, Patricia H. Hinchey

FORTHCOMING
Bilingual Education, Rosa Castro Feinberg

CONTEMPORARY EDUCATION ISSUES

Migrant Education

➤ A Reference Handbook

Judith A. Gouwens

A B C ❦ C L I O

Santa Barbara, California • Denver, Colorado • Oxford, England

Library of Congress Cataloging-in-Publication Data

Gouwens, Judith A.
    Migrant education : a reference handbook / Judith A. Gouwens.
        p.   cm. — (Contemporary education issues)
    Includes bibliographical references and index.
        ISBN 1-57607-338-6 (hardcover : alk. paper); 1-57607-555-9 (e-book)
    1. Children of migrant laborers—Education—United States—Handbooks, manuals, etc.   I. Title.   II. Series.
        LC5151.G68   2001
        371.826'24—dc21   2001005060

This book is also available on the World Wide Web as an e-book.
Visit www.abc-clio.com for details.

07 06 05 04 03 02 01   10 9 8 7 6 5 4 3 2 1

ABC-CLIO, Inc.
130 Cremona Drive, P.O. Box 1911
Santa Barbara, California 93116-1911

This book is printed on acid-free paper ⊗.
Manufactured in the United States of America

This book is dedicated to migrant educators throughout the United States who believe in the tremendous potential of migrant children and youth, who expect migrant children and youth to reach that potential, and who work diligently to break down the barriers that stand in the way.

✦ Contents

✨ Series Editor's Preface

The Contemporary Education Issues series is dedicated to providing readers with an up-to-date exploration of the central issues in education today. Books in the series will examine such controversial topics as home schooling, charter schools, privatization of public schools, Native American education, African American education, literacy, curriculum development, and many others. The series is national in scope and is intended to encourage research by anyone interested in the field.

Because education is undergoing radical if not revolutionary change, the series is particularly concerned with how contemporary controversies in education affect both the organization of schools and the content and delivery of curriculum. Authors will endeavor to provide a balanced understanding of the issues and their effects on teachers, students, parents, administrators, and policymakers. The aim of the Contemporary Education Issues series is to publish excellent research on today's educational concerns by some of the finest scholar/practitioners in the field while pointing to new directions. The series promises to offer important analyses of some of the most controversial issues facing society today.

Danny Weil
Series Editor

✏ Preface

Writing this book about migrant education provided me with the opportunity to reflect back on my own experiences with migrant families and migrant education, first as a teacher and later as a consultant and provider of technical assistance to migrant educators. This work has made me more aware of the problems migrant families face, and of the incredible commitment of migrant educators to address those problems.

As an elementary teacher in Michigan, I worked with many migrant children and their families. In my school district, the Migrant Education Program had several ways of addressing the barriers migrant children face. Bilingual teacher assistants in classrooms offered opportunities for additional instruction, which helped to fill the gaps in children's education left by moving from school to school. Assistants also helped by translating lessons into Spanish so that migrant students could understand. Teacher assistants and other staff members of the Migrant Education Program also facilitated communication between the school and the families, translating when necessary and mediating when the cultural gap between the classroom and the home was too great for teachers and parents to negotiate by themselves. The migrant education staff also assisted in the timely transfer of educational and medical records. They helped families access needed medical, dental, and social services. I drew on this support system regularly as I worked with migrant children and their families.

I was always impressed with the strength and resilience of these families and the hopes and expectations the parents had for their children. One of the migrant families with whom I worked exemplifies the commitment to their children's educational success that I saw in so many of the families. This family had decided that the mother would stay in Michigan with the children, so that their education would not be disrupted, while the father migrated with the crops and the available work. The oldest child in the family, Juan, was six years old and in my first-grade classroom. Juan had six younger siblings, one of whom was in kindergarten. While the father was out of state working, the mother was responsible for the care not only of her own seven young children but also for two children of relatives who traveled with her husband to find work.

The mother was left without transportation—the father needed the family truck to travel—or access to child care that would provide her with any respite from the nine children in her care. She had no friends or relatives in the area who could help her with the children or serve as a support system for her. Juan and his kindergarten-aged brother were often charged with watching the younger children while their mother shopped for groceries or did the laundry at a nearby Laundromat. In spite of their family responsibilities, the two boys had regular school attendance and did well academically. Although she was very busy caring for nine children, the mother was supportive of the boys' learning. She regularly read with the boys, and it was obvious when talking with her that she carefully monitored the papers and other work that Juan took home.

Caring for so many children provided obvious challenges. The boys were often not clean, and their clothes smelled badly enough that other children often commented about the odor and refused to sit near or play with the boys. The family had no telephone, and the mother did not visit the school during the school day or attend regular parent-teacher conferences. Since she could not come to the school, I went to visit her at home to talk with her about the odor problem.

Even during my visit, the mother was busy with the children. As we talked, she fed and diapered babies, comforted toddlers, and directed the children away from activities that could be harmful. I observed Juan and his next-younger sibling as they also cared for the younger children. As the mother and I talked, I learned a great deal about the commitment of a young mother to the children in her care and the difficulties she faced being their sole caregiver twenty-four hours a day, seven days a week. I also saw Juan in a different light, understanding the responsibilities placed on him as the oldest child in the house. I found out that all the children's dirty clothes, including wet and soiled cloth diapers, were put in bags and baskets together until the weekly trip to the Laundromat. Sometimes there were not enough clean clothes for the boys to wear; at those times, they wore clothes that had been in the bags and baskets of dirty clothes—hence the odor.

With the support of the Migrant Education Program, in coordination with the local county health department and the owner of the house in which the family lived, a washer and dryer were installed in the house so that clothing could be laundered at home and more often. Provisions were made for Head Start placements for the preschoolers and child care for the infants so that the mother would have some time for herself. Like so many other migrant families, this mother had no idea that such support was available to her family, and did not know how to access it. For her and for her children, the Migrant Education Program provided a critical support system that affected her entire family.

As a technical assistance provider, I worked with migrant educators in several states, through professional development workshops, presentations at migrant education conferences, and summer migrant program sites. I had the opportunity to visit migrant camps and to observe migrant families working in the fields.

I met migrant educators who were enthusiastically committed to the success of the children they served and worked far beyond the hours for which they were paid to help the children learn. I met migrant educators also committed to providing fun activities to migrant children and their families. In many communities, migrant educators visited each migrant camp several evenings during the summer to have picnics and parties for the families. The educators made sure that the children had opportunities to go swimming and fishing during the summer and to visit museums and other places of interest.

In one state, I visited migrant workers as they harvested *pepinos,* the tiny cucumbers that would be used to make the smallest pickles. On their hands and knees, the pickers crawled between rows of prickly cucumber plants from dawn until dusk, filling sacks that they dragged behind them along the rows. In the evening, I met teenagers who picked pepinos all day and went to school after they left the fields to accrue the credits necessary for them to keep up with classmates in their home schools. Bone-tired, they studied nonetheless, because they wanted to graduate from high school.

In April 2001, I attended the National Migrant Education Conference, sponsored annually by the National Association of State Directors of Migrant Education (NASDME). The conference, held in 2001 in Kissimmee, Florida, brought together migrant educators, migrant parents, and migrant students from across the United States to share their successes and concerns and to celebrate the thirty-fifth anniversary of the Migrant Education Program. At the conference, I met a migrant parent who, along with her children, is benefiting from the Migrant Education Program. This mother, from a remote native community in Alaska, was offered a position as a teacher assistant in the Migrant Education Program at her children's school. As she worked in the program, she was encouraged to continue her own education. She is now enrolled in a teacher education program at the University of Alaska, accessible to her because much of the program is offered online. Her three sons, all participants in the Migrant Education Program at some time during their schooling, are following the model set for them by their mother. They all have career plans that involve higher education. Two of the young men are full-time college students; the third is still in high school. This mother speaks enthusiastically about how the Migrant Education Program has made a difference in the lives of her whole family.

The first chapter of this book discusses what it means to be migrant in the United States and the barriers to education that migrant farmworkers and their children face. Subsequent chapters describe the historical development of the Migrant Education Program in the United States, how the Migrant Education Program is currently being implemented, and how some programs are using innovative strategies and techniques to address the barriers that traditionally impede the educational success of migrant students.

In the United States, migrant farmworkers and their children remain largely invisible. Few people understand how important these workers are to the U.S. economy or how many of these workers live in poverty. And few people understand how difficult it is for the children of these migrant farmworkers to access the education that is so crucial to helping them break the poverty cycle. It is my hope that this book will contribute to making these people more visible and to acknowledging the very important roles that migrant education and educators play in the lives and future success of these children and youth.

Judith A. Gouwens

✒ Acknowledgments

I would like to thank the many migrant educators who provided information and guidance throughout this project: the U.S. Office of Migrant Education, Department of Education; the National Association of State Directors of Migrant Education and its former president, Angela Branz-Spall, the Montana director of Migrant Education; Susan Duron, national consultant to migrant programs; Migrant Education Program directors from other states who shared information about innovative migrant programs in their states; Brenda Pessin, education director of the Illinois Migrant Council; the staff of the summer migrant program in Leipsic, Ohio; Glenn P. Johnston, director of the Florida Migrant Education Summer Institute; Peggy Wimberley from the Migrant Student Program at the University of Texas at Austin; the Migrant Education Program staff of the Lower Kuskokwim School District in Bethel, Alaska; Don McBride and Becky Smith, Missouri Migrant Education consultants; Margaret Walpole, Kathi Van Soest, and Mary Ellen Good, from the Centennial BOCES in Greeley, Colorado; the Migrant Education Program staff of Garden City, Kansas; Tawni Helms, Judy Jacobson, and their colleagues from Best S.E.L.F.; Nora Oranday, the media and education consultant at the Mexican Cultural and Educational Institute of Chicago; other migrant educators and parents who talked with me about the importance of the Migrant Education Program to the success of migrant children and youth; and the migrant students themselves who shared their eloquent writing about the migrant experience. I also would like to thank Mary and Fred Schutmaat, who helped me with translations from Spanish to English, and Pamella Myers, a former student and friend, who helped to gather background information for this book, read drafts, and provided moral support.

Most of all, I would like to thank my life partner and best friend, Thomas Gouwens, for all of his support, encouragement, and feedback throughout the project. His patience and love always help me to persevere!

Chapter One

●← Introduction

IF MY CAP COULD TALK

IF MY CAP COULD TALK,
>   It would share many secrets that few know.
>   It would tell about my travels through Oklahoma, Oregon, Idaho and Utah,
>   It would shout of my final destination—"Washington!"
>   It would brag about the caverns and tourist sites that I passed by, the Delta Center in Utah, the Denver Bronco Stadium and the Rocky Mountains.

IF MY CAP COULD TALK,
>   It would probably tell of the volcano that I lived close by,
>   And the Canadian border that was so close to the place I called home.
>   It would tell about all the waterfalls I saw.

IF MY CAP COULD TALK,
>   It would tell about the sunrises and sunsets that I really got to see.

YOU SEE IF MY CAP COULD TALK,
>   It would share many secrets that few know.
>   It would tell about my travels, the caverns and the tourist sights I passed by but did not visit.
>   It would proudly tell of the volcano and Canadian border I knew was there, but I did not see.
>   It would tell about the waterfalls I saw from afar but could not feel.

IF MY CAP COULD TALK,
>   It would tell about my life as a migrant and how hard I had to work.
>   It would sadly tell about how tired I got and of how sometimes I was cold.
>   It would quietly talk about how hard it was for me to walk on my knees all day.
>   It would talk about the blisters and the bruises that I got while working.
>   It would proudly talk about how hard I worked, how I missed home and even school.

IF MY CAP COULD TALK,
> It would share my dreams to graduate, go to college and become an accountant.
> Because I want to visit the Denver Bronco Stadium and watch a game; to experience a real waterfall and walk on a volcano; and to travel and get to be a real tourist.

—Julio Gaona,[1] aged 16
Corpus Christi, Texas

Migrant children and youth have many opportunities to learn life's lessons about hard work, about being tired and cold, about blisters and bruises, about missing home and friends and school. At the same time, they miss so many other life lessons and experiences, and they often struggle to learn the academic lessons that are so important to their future success. The migrant population ranks as the most educationally disadvantaged in the United States, making the education of the children and families of migrant workers in the United States a critical issue. Of all groups of children in the country, those of migrant farmworkers are the most undereducated and the least likely to complete high school and go on to postsecondary education. In addition, these children rank among the highest in the United States in rates of poverty and malnutrition and have the least access to health care.

These factors combine with high rates of mobility from school to school and its accompanying educational discontinuity, the language barriers many migrant families face, and the social and cultural isolation they experience, to put these children and youth at great risk of academic failure. Many of these children and youth engage in strenuous physical labor, either alone or with their families. This work further interferes with the education of migrant children and youth through fatigue from the labor and absences from school to work, an economic necessity for many migrant families and the growing number of migrant youth who travel alone.

This chapter provides a picture of who migrant workers in the United States are. It also describes the conditions of being migrant and of migrant labor that interfere with or have the potential to interfere with the educational success of migrant children, youth, and families. Subsequent chapters describe how this issue has been addressed historically, and how the U.S. Department of Education, the government of Mexico, state departments of education, school districts, schools, and other agencies and organizations have intervened in the past and are intervening currently to break the cycle of educational disadvantage experienced by many migrant children and youth.

WHO ARE MIGRANT WORKERS IN THE UNITED STATES?

> As migrants we were seekers who were searching and learning about ourselves as we migrated from state to state looking for seasonal labor. It was no accident that we learned so much about life, because we were constantly seeking new opportunities.   (Chahin 1998, 120)

Migrant workers in the United States are generally considered to be seasonal workers in agriculture, fishing, forestry, and plant nurseries; they travel from job to job as the seasons change and as work becomes available. Some of them travel from state to state, others from work site to work site within one state, and still others travel from Mexico and other countries to the United States for work and then back to their home countries. There are several sources of information about such workers in the United States.

The U.S. Department of Agriculture (USDA) defines hired farmworkers as "employed persons who . . . [do] farmwork for cash wages or salary. . . . Hired farmworkers include persons who manage farms for employers on a paid basis, supervisors of farmworkers, and farm and nursery workers" (Runyan 1998, 19). The USDA further classifies farmworkers according to the industry in which they are employed. These categories include

- ➡ Crop production—establishments primarily engaged in producing crops, plants, vines, and trees (excluding forestry operations)
- ➡ Livestock production—establishments primarily engaged in the keeping, grazing, or feeding of livestock, and
- ➡ Other agricultural establishments—establishments primarily engaged in agricultural services, forestry, fishing, hunting, trapping, landscape and horticultural services, and other agriculture-related establishments (Runyan 1998, 19)

In its profile of farmworkers from 1990 to 1996, the USDA does not provide data specifically for migrant farmworkers, and mentions only that "some hired farmworkers migrate from production area to production area during several months of the year" (Runyan 1998, 1).

The data on farmworkers are impossible to disaggregate or compare because there is little agreement at the federal government level on the definition of *migrant*. The failure to coin and use a consistent definition makes it difficult to compare data from study to study or from government agencies, or to track migrant population over time. Data reported by various agencies and sources in the federal government differ widely, but all sources report that there are large numbers of migrant workers in the workforce of the United States.

The U.S. Department of Labor periodically conducts one of the few studies of worker characteristics that specifically addresses migrant workers. This study, the National Agriculture Workers Survey (NAWS), defines migrants as workers who "travel seventy-five miles or more in search of crop work." This study was based on interviews with a large sample of farmworkers across the country. Martin reported that data extrapolated from the study conducted between 1989 and 1991 suggest that there were about 840,000 farmworkers that matched the study's definition (Martin 1996, 21). According to Martin, data from the survey showed the following demographics of migrant workers. Migrant workers were

- Primarily Hispanic (94 percent)
- Born in Mexico (80 percent)
- Married, with children (52 percent)
- Doing farm work in the United States without their families (59 percent)
- Mostly men (82 percent), and
- Are today, or were until 1987–1988, unauthorized workers (67 percent) (Martin 1996, 21)

The study also estimated that between 1989 and 1991, approximately 409,000 children traveled with these migrant laborers, and about 36,000 of those children traveling also did farm work (Martin 1996, 22). In 1998, the number of migrant children identified by the states as being eligible for migrant education was considerably larger; but because different definitions of "migrant" were used to generate the data, it is impossible to know whether the differences in numbers result from differing definitions or from a growing migrant population.

The eighth NAWS study (U.S. Department of Labor 2000), which reports data gathered during 1997 and 1998, provides updated and additional information about farm labor. The data in the report describe migrant workers who work directly with crops. According to this study, 56 percent of all farmworkers in the United States migrate to find work. This includes 39 percent considered to be "shuttle migrants," or those who move between two or more jobs at a location far from their home bases; and 17 percent labeled "follow the crop" migrants, or those working at two or more farm jobs more than seventy-five miles apart. Forty-two percent of the farmworkers interviewed in the study maintain a home outside the United States (U.S. Department of Labor 2000, 21).

In the 1997–1998 sample, 90 percent of migrant workers reported that they were born outside the United States. The median age for "follow the crop" workers was twenty-six; "shuttle" migrants reported a median age of twenty-seven (U.S. Department of Labor 2000, 21). The study also asked workers about their authorization to work in the United States; 52 percent of all farmworkers interviewed were unauthorized, a porportion that is increasing by about 1 percent per year. Although this data was not disaggregated by migrant status, one can assume that the majority of migrant farmworkers were not authorized to work in the United States (U.S. Department of Labor 2000, 21, 22).

The study looked at how many weeks migrant farmworkers were employed in farm labor. New migrants (those having less than one year's experience in U.S. agriculture) worked an average of only seventeen weeks a year, but those with more experience worked about twenty-six weeks a year (U.S. Department of Labor 2000, 22). The demand for farm labor in the United States has been decreasing in recent years, according to the study, and the farm workforce is considerably underemployed. In July, for example, a month when farm labor peaks, only 56 percent of the available farm labor force was employed in 1997 and 1998 (U.S. Department of Labor 2000, 25).

A study of migrant demographics reported by the U.S. General Accounting Office provided additional demographic information about migrant families. According to that study, most migrant farmworkers are younger than thirty-five; indeed, the population of "teenage boys, some as young as thirteen . . . [who] migrate without families has continued to increase" (U.S. GAO 1999, 4).

The U.S. Department of Agriculture (USDA) publishes quarterly reports on farm labor. For purposes of these reports, the USDA defines a migrant worker as "a farm worker whose employment required travel that prevented the farm worker from returning to his/her permanent place of residence the same day" (NASS 2000, 10). The USDA August 18, 2000, report on farm labor shows that a significant number of farm laborers could be classified as migrant. According to that report, from 1997 to 2000, between 6 and 13.7 percent of all hired farmworkers were migrants by the USDA's definition. Table 1.1 shows the percent of hired farmworkers who were migrant (by the USDA definition) by quarter during that period. The same USDA report indicates that during that period there were a total of 1.24 million farm laborers; applying the percentages of migrant farmworkers shown in the table yields between

74,400 (6 percent) and 169,880 (13.7 percent) migrant farm laborers in the United States.

These totals represent workers who register with the U.S. Department of Agriculture or whose employers do so on their behalf. The totals do not include workers who do not register or whose employers do not register them, nor are they likely to provide accurate data about those who are undocumented. Runyan noted that "undocumented foreign farmworkers may, because of their illegal status, avoid survey enumerators" (Runyan 1998, 2). The NAWS study (U.S. Department of Labor 2000) reported significantly higher percentages of migrant farmworkers, perhaps because the sample of workers interviewed were not specifically drawn from the population of USDA registered farmworkers. If the proportion of migrant farmworkers reported in the NAWS study, 56 percent, is accurate, there may be more than 694,000 migrant farmworkers in the United States.

Kindler (1995) reports that migrant workers are employed in all forty-nine of the continental United States, the District of Columbia, and Puerto Rico. In addition the state of Hawaii began identifying a population of migrating farmworkers in 1998. Traditionally, the migration of farmworkers and fishers in the United States has generally followed one of three routes, or streams, across the country as crops are ready for harvest or as fishing seasons occur. The streams are labeled the Eastern Stream, the Central Stream, and the Western Stream. The Eastern Stream includes states in the south and along the East Coast. The Central Stream begins in Texas and extends northward through the plains states and into California. The Western Stream begins in Southern California and extends north along the West Coast. States that are included in each of the streams are listed in Table 1.2.

The traditional migration patterns led to the classification of states as home-base or sending states and receiving states. Home-base states (or sending states) "are those where many migrant families live for all or most of the year, depending on whether they migrate within one state or between states. . . . Receiving states are those in which most migrants work for a few weeks or months per year and then return home" (Kindler 1995, 7).

But migration patterns have been changing since the 1980s. These changes "reflect the increased agricultural work; growth of large-scale agribusiness, including poultry and hog farming; the rotation of workers from harvest work to other types of agricultural work; and increased opportunities for jobs in other types of seasonal rural jobs, particularly the recreation industry" (U.S. GAO 6, 7).

There are migrant workers who still follow the traditional

TABLE 1.1 Migrant Workers: Percent of All Hired Workers, United States, by Quarter (Includes Agricultural Service Workers), 1997–2000

	January	*April*	*July*	*October*
1997	9.5	6.3	10.8	11.2
1998	7.3	6.6	13.7	11.0
1999	6.0	8.7	12.4	12.3
2000	7.7	8.5	11.5[a]	11.9

[a]Revised.
SOURCE: National Agricultural Statistics Service Report on Farm Labor, November 2000: 12.

TABLE 1.2 Migrant Streams

Eastern Stream	*Central Stream*	*Western Stream*
Alabama	Arkansas	Alaska
Connecticut	Illinois	Arizona
Delaware	Indiana	California
Florida	Iowa	Colorado
Georgia	Kansas	Idaho
Kentucky	Louisiana	Montana
Maine	Michigan	Nevada
Maryland	Minnesota	New Mexico
Massachusetts	Missouri	Oregon
Mississippi	Nebraska	Utah
New Hampshire	North Dakota	Washington
New Jersey	Ohio	Wyoming
New York	Oklahoma	
North Carolina	South Dakota	
Pennsylvania	Texas	
Rhode Island	Wisconsin	
South Carolina		
Tennessee		
Vermont		
Virginia		
West Virginia		
District of Columbia		
Puerto Rico		

SOURCE: Kindler 1995: 3.

streams, but there are also migrant workers who migrate from work site to work site with no home base, and others who follow no specific pattern in migration. Children from one Texas school district, for example, traveled during the 1997–1998 school year "from their home base, attended schools in at least forty other states, and then returned home" (U.S. GAO 1999, 6).

Many migrant workers come from outside the United States. The 1993 NAWS study reported that "about 700,000 workers shuttled into the United States from homes abroad, usually in Mexico" (Martin 1996, 21). But it is difficult to speculate on the accuracy of that number because many of those who migrate from Mexico are undocumented.

Many migrants are considered intrastate; that is, they travel between work sites within a given state. The Migrant Education Program in the state of Alaska, for example, serves children from families who are all considered intrastate migrants and involved in the fishing industry; these families migrate only within Alaska. In Hawaii, where migrant education is a relatively new program, having begun in the summer of 1999, migrants are not only intrastate but are also intra-island; that is, they migrate between plantation and agricultural sites on a particular island.

Most migrant families move more than once each year. A survey of 1993–1994 Migrant Head Start parents found that the majority (67 percent) of migrant farmworker families lived in two or three locations each year. Twenty-two percent lived in only one location, and 11 percent lived in four or more locations. (U.S. GAO 1999, 4).

Chavkin analyzed the demographic data of migrant workers and found that migrant workers were members of a variety of ethnic groups. His analysis shows that migrant workers in the Eastern Stream include Anglos, Puerto Ricans, African Americans, Jamaican and Haitian Blacks, and Mexican Americans and Mexican nationals. Migrant workers in the Central Stream include Mexican Americans and Mexican nationals, and "small numbers" of Native Americans. The Western Stream is made up primarily of Mexican Americans and Mexican nationals, as well as Southeast Asians (Chavkin 1996, 326). That the majority of migrant workers is Hispanic belies the great diversity of this part of the American labor force. The U.S. General Accounting Office reports that "the migrant labor force continues to include English-speaking, white U.S. families picking blueberries in Maine; women bikers (motorcyclists) picking fruit in Idaho; Bengali-speaking workers harvesting grapes and other fruit in California; Russian-speaking workers fishing and logging in the Northwest; and Gullah-speaking, African American families shrimping in Georgia" (U.S. GAO 1999, 4). There are also native peoples in Alaska who work in fishing and lumbering, and native Hawaiians working on plantations in Hawaii.

Migrant labor has played a significant role in the United States workforce for many years. Takaki, who describes the use of migrant labor in agriculture in the middle of the nineteenth century and in building the railroads as early as the 1880s, notes that "railroad construction work was migratory. Railroad workers and their families literally lived in boxcars and were shunted to the places where they were needed" (Takaki 1993, 185). These migrant workers were typically ethnic minorities (Mexican, Japanese, and Chinese) and part of a caste system that placed them at the bottom in terms of the labor pool and the scale of economics. Supervisors and middle-level personnel were all Anglo; the most menial laborers were Mexicans and other minorities. And even when the work was equal, the Mexicans and other minority laborers were paid less than their nonminority coworkers (Takaki 1993, 187).

By the turn of the twentieth century, Mexicans were being encouraged to migrate to the United States to fill the increasing need for labor in agriculture, the railroads, food-processing plants, and other industries (Takaki 1993, 321). But during times when the U.S. economy was not as strong, they were deported. Romo reports that "during the Great Depression, when labor demands fell off and the labor supply in the Southwest went up as U.S. migrants arrived from the dust bowl, some 500,000 Mexicans—many of them born in the United States and U.S. citizens—were repatriated to Mexico. . . . In the 1950s, over a million Mexicans were again deported in Operation Wetback" (Romo 1996, 63).

The impact of migrant labor on the United States economy is large. According to Schlosser, "Nearly every head of lettuce, every bunch of grapes, every avocado, peach, and plum" consumed in the United States is picked by hand, mostly by migrant laborers (Schlosser 1995, 82). Without such migrant labor, fresh vegetables and fruit, a diet staple in the United States, would be either much more expensive or unavailable.

In his interview study of migrant laborers, Rothenberg quotes Salvador Moreno as he described the lack of security in migrant labor:

> There's no security in farmwork. Most jobs are temporary and often you can only find work during the harvest. When the harvest ends, the work stops. As the harvest is ending, you start wondering, "Now, what will I do? How will I find another job? Where should I go": There are always people telling you about some town where another harvest is about to start. . . . If you go, you never know what you'll be doing or what it will really be like. (Rothenberg 1998, 8)

Migrant farmworkers continue to be among the lowest paid workers in the United States. The November 2000 National Agricultural Statistics Service *Farm Labor Report* reported that the average wage for farmworkers was $7.74 per hour, an increase of 43 cents over the previous year (NASS 2000, 1). Migrant and seasonal farmworkers, according to Martin (1996), typically work about 1,000 hours per year and make less money than other farmworkers. Even at the average rate reported by the National Agricultural Statistics Service report, annual income for these workers would total $7,740, well below the poverty level. The average annual income for a migrant worker may in reality be much lower. Migrant families often work together and receive only one wage; that wage could be compensation for as many as two adults and several children. In his interview with Rothenberg, Jose Martinez described working as a child.

> Until we were old enough to work legally, we'd get paid under the names of older family members. We needed the money and me and all my brothers were an essential part of our family's economy. We all contributed. . . . Working was what we did to survive. It didn't matter that it was illegal. (Rothenberg 1998, 273)

Rothenberg reported that in 1996, some documented farmworkers made as little as $3,500 (Rothenberg 1998, 6). Wages for undocumented workers could be even lower.

The 2000 NAWS study does not disaggregate income data by migrant status; it does report that nearly 75 percent of farmworker families in the United States earned less that $10,000 annually in 1997 and 1998, and that half of all farmworkers earned less than $7,500. About 60 percent of single farmworkers and those who were married and the parents of children earned incomes below the poverty line (U.S. Department of Labor 2000, 39). The study also compared real purchasing power and found that while the average hourly wage paid to farmworkers had increased in 1998 to $6.18, real buying power had decreased by more than 10 percent (U.S. Department of Labor 2000, 33). Given that migrant farmworkers work fewer weeks each year than their nonmigrating counterparts, and that foreign-born farmworkers were "considerably more likely to be impoverished than those born in the United States (65 percent vs. 42 percent)"(U.S. Department of Labor 2000, 39), it stands to reason that many migrant incomes fall far below the average for all farmworkers. In addition, few farmworkers receive fringe benefits, and only 5 percent of those interviewed in 1997 and 1998 reported that their employers provided health insurance (U.S. Department of Labor 2000, 36).

The migrant labor force in the United States includes many children and youth. In testimony before the Select Committee on Children, Youth, and Families, the Farmworker Justice Fund estimated in 1990 that children perform as much as 25 percent of farm labor in the United States.

> My parents work in *la fresa* [the strawberries] and *la mora* [the raspberries], and my mom sometimes packs mushrooms. During the week, they leave in the morning around six o'clock. I go and help them,

mostly on weekends. I help pick the strawberries and put them in boxes. Last year my father took me to the fields a lot during the week, too, instead of bringing me to school. (Rios, 1993, 12)

These children and youth are either not protected by the Fair Labor Standards Act (FLSA) or they are working on farms where the standards of the FLSA are not enforced. In addition, many activities that are prohibited for children under eighteen in other industries are legal in agriculture. Davis states: "In agriculture, fourteen-year-olds can work for unlimited hours and sixteen-year-olds can perform even hazardous jobs—operating heavy equipment, working on a 20-foot ladder, or handling pesticides (FLSA, 29 U.S.C.§213[a][6])" (Davis 1997, 1). The FLSA permits younger children to work along with their parents if the work is performed outside school hours, and farm owners are often unwilling to prohibit child labor in their fields. Elvia, a high school student from Pharr, Texas, and a participant in the summer migrant education program in Hoopeston, Illinois, writes about the frustration she feels when she detassels corn:

> DETASSELING
> Detasseling was hard for
> Elvia
> Today, she was
> Angry and
> Sad at the
> Same time she had to
> Elevate herself to reach and
> Loosen the
> Inseparable tassel from the tall corn stalk
> No one was there to help and she had to
> Get going because she had more detasseling
> to do so she tried her best and took it out
> with all her might
> (Elvia 2000, 16)

For many migrant families, their children's work is necessary if the family is to earn enough money to subsist, and children are sometimes kept out of school to work with their families. Sometimes even very young children are in the fields because their parents cannot afford or have no access to child care. And a substantial and increasing number of youths migrate on their own to work. Davis notes that "the health and well-being of children and adolescents who work in agriculture are jeopardized by the long hours of labor and dangerous working conditions" (Davis 1997, 1).

It is not only young migrant workers who are subjected to unsafe working and living conditions. In spite of the 1983 Migrant and Seasonal Agricultural Worker Protection Act, which was designed to address issues of pay, working conditions, and work-related conditions of migrant and seasonal farmworkers, many migrant workers also live in substandard housing and work under conditions that are hazardous to their health.

Part of living below the poverty line for migrant families is the inadequate housing available in most places where they work. Isabel Valle traveled with a migrant family for a year, documenting their lives and the issues they faced as they migrated. She described living conditions of many migrant families as "deplorable." One member of the family Valle traveled with described housing conditions at a migrant camp in Michigan:

> I remember when we first got there I looked around and I said, "Look at all those chicken coops!" Then the farmer told us that was where we were living. . . . It was dirty. There were a few portable toilets for quite a lot of people and they were always filled to the top. I knew I was going to get sick. (Valle 1994, 21)

In this same migrant camp, the only bathing facility was a crude outdoor shower with no plumbing; water was carried in buckets from the so-called houses to an enclosure made by sheets hung at one corner of the fence.

Although local, state, and federal officials inspect migrant housing, it is still substandard in some places. The 1983 Migrant and Seasonal Farmworker Protection Act (MSFPA) put in place standards for worker housing. These standards require that housing be registered and inspected regularly. Before these standards were enacted, growers often provided housing to workers free of charge or at nominal rates during the time they were working at that site.

> Following lawsuits, investigations, fines, and bad publicity, many growers decided to close down or even demolish the housing they had previously provided to workers. Since migrant laborers still need temporary housing, they were forced to find rental housing or live in illegal labor camps. . . . In areas with a high concentration of seasonal farmworkers, it is not uncommon to find old trailers or crumbling shacks rented to farm laborers at exorbitant weekly rates. (Rothenberg 1998, 114)

Growers who do maintain housing for workers may be able to get around the standards set by the MSFPA by having their facilities inspected before the migrant workers arrive. Once the housing is approved, growers allow more occupants to move in than the housing is approved for or fail to make repairs of plumbing or other basic systems when they break down.

Agricultural migrant workers can be exposed to high levels of pesticides, fertilizers, and other chemicals used in agriculture. According to Leon's 1996 study of migrant health conditions, exposure to these chemicals results in "potential risks of having children with birth defects or . . . cancer or other illnesses" (Leon 1996, 1).

In addition to such issues as HIV, substance abuse, and teen pregnancy, also prevalent in the general population, migrant families experience various other health issues. Migrant health issues cited by Leon are those generally associated with poverty, high mobility, poor sanitation, crowded living conditions, and limited access to health care services. They include malnutrition, higher rates of infectious diseases, including those that are sexually transmitted, than the general population, and a tuberculosis rate that is twenty times higher than that of the general population (Leon 1996, 3, 7–8). Although there is a network of federally funded migrant clinics, access may be limited by factors that include inconvenience, language barriers, undocumented status, and lack of information about availability.

HOW DO THE CONDITIONS OF MIGRANT LABOR PUT MIGRANT CHILDREN, YOUTH, AND FAMILIES AT RISK OF EDUCATIONAL FAILURE?

Several factors complicate the education of migrant children, youth, and adults. Chief among those factors are the effects of mobility. Migrant families move as farm labor is needed and work is available, often from south to north in the spring and summer, and back south again in late summer and fall, with the crops. Children of migrant farmworkers may move several times and attend several schools during each school year. Migrant families often have a home base where they typically spend the winter months, and a home school, often referred to as a sending school. In most cases, the families move before the school year ends; this means taking their children out of school before the end of the term, and either keeping the children out of school or enrolling them in new schools, referred to as receiving schools, as they travel. When they return to their home bases, migrant children often miss the beginning of the school year because they have enrolled at their home-base schools several weeks or even months after a new fall term has begun.

Further complications of such mobility arise from the difficulties involved in transferring children's school records from one school to another. Records of children who move from school to school are often incomplete and they offer little, if any, information that can help schools provide appropriate educational services to these mobile students. The transfer of student records can be a slow process, and many times by the time records have been transferred, children have moved on to yet other schools. In other cases, children have been assigned to programs or grade levels incorrectly, or have had to endure lengthy diagnostic processes before being appropriately assigned, thereby missing precious instructional time.

Curriculum that differs greatly from state to state and from one school to another, even within a given state, is also a factor that places migrant children and youth at risk of educational failure. Because of differences in curriculum and in the content and sequence of instruction, migrant children and youth often miss critical content and instruction; these omissions leave gaps in schooling and can result in migrant children's failure to keep up with their age groups, and in high school, failure to accrue enough credits to graduate.

An additional complication of the transfer from one school to another is that many migrants have their home bases outside the United States. Schools in Mexico, for example, differ in significant ways from schools in the United States. As they are in the United States, all Mexicans are entitled to a free, secular education. In Mexico, this education is guaranteed by The General Law of Education enacted in 1993. In contrast to the educational system in the United States, the Mexican education system is nationalized. The organization of the schools, the curriculum, and, to a large extent, the funding, are standardized throughout the country.

Free public education in Mexico begins with initial education for children from forty-five days to three years of age. From age four, and continuing for two years (and in some private schools, three years), children attend preschool, the first formal education program. Primary schools are divided into lower grades (first through third) and higher grades (fourth through sixth). Secondary school (seventh through ninth grades) has only been a part of basic education in Mexico since the 1993 General Law. States are expected to provide access to secondary education for students who "acquire the right" to go on to secondary school, but many students do not go on to secondary schools (Andrade de Herrera 1996, 42–48). Mexico has addressed the issue of children whose families migrate within Mexico by establishing a primary program specifically for migrant students in the fourteen states among which most interstate migration occurs (Andrade de Herrera 1996, 48).

Although the larger percentage of the funding for secondary schools comes from individual states, and states have the responsibility for administering schools, under the decentralization that was part of the 1993 General Law of Education, the curriculum remains nationalized. Programs of study are published for each level of schooling, beginning with the initial education, and specific time distributions are delineated for all primary and secondary schools. The initial education focuses on preparing children for preschool and teaching mothers parenting skills. Curriculum in the preschool includes "mathematics, oral and written language, artistic sensibility, nature study, and development of psycho-motor abilities" (Andrade de Herrera 1996, 43). Primary schools have four-hour school days and a 200-day school year, the major part of each school day being devoted to Spanish written and oral communication and mathematics. The curriculum for first and second grades also includes Knowledge of the Environment, which integrates the natural and social sciences, artistic education, and physical education. In the third through sixth grades, in addition to Spanish and mathematics, the curriculum includes natural sciences, history, geography, civic education, artistic education, and physical education. The secondary school curriculum is also prescribed; it includes Spanish, mathematics, world history, the history of Mexico, general geography, the geography of Mexico, education orientation, civics, biology, physics, chemistry, foreign language, artistic expression and appreciation, physical education, and technological education (Andrade de Herrera 1996, 49).

Textbooks written to support the programs of study for primary schools are published by the federal government and provided to students free of charge. Standard textbooks are also required for secondary schools; these textbooks are published by private publishers after a review by the federal government, and then they are included on a list of approved texts. At the secondary level, textbooks are not provided free of charge. The federal government also publishes teaching manuals and provides professional development for teachers at all levels (Andrade de Herrera 1996, 42–49).

The organization and curriculum are not the only components of Mexican education that differ from education in the United States. José Macías studied instructional practice in Mexican primary schools and found it was different in significant ways from instruction in U.S. schools. In his observations of primary school classrooms, Macías noted that

> teachers directed the instructional process in this general sequence: (a) explicit, detailed presentation of task and directions, typically involving

reading of narrative text, (b) elicitation of group and individual (often becoming group) student response, and (c) scribe notebook exercises or other projects requiring visual and hands-on student creativity. High levels of interaction characterized the instructional exchange between teachers and students as well as among students. Put another way, teachers formally directed the instructional process, but informally motivated student activity and collaboration. Talk and interchange throughout formed the social basis of that process. (Macías 1992, 19)

Macías observed that instruction in primary classrooms in Mexico tolerates and even encourages high levels of student-initiated discourse, both between students and teachers and between and among students; this is in contrast to classrooms in the United States, where a "teacher-to-individual pupil and vice versa, task-oriented cycle of interaction predominates" (Macías 1992, 14). He argued that this difference is shaped by school and home social and cultural expectations, and that for children who migrate between Mexican and U.S. classrooms, "the struggle of making a transition from one socioculturally shaped institutional experience to a new one" is a fundamental part of the discontinuity these students experience (Macías 1992, 14).

In addition, some of the children from outside the United States may not have attended school at all in their home countries. These children and youth enter schools in the United States with no understanding at all of the educational process, and often without academic knowledge and/or literacy in their first language. Not only do they not understand the culture and language of the school but they also lack the academic preparation needed for placement in classrooms with children of their own ages; and so they miss the socialization that is so important to students' feeling they belong.

School attendance is an additional factor related to the mobility of migrant children and youth. Migrant children and youth miss valuable days of instruction as they travel with their families from one work site to the next. If the family is at a work site for only a short time, parents may not enroll children in school at all. But even when they are enrolled, migrant children and youth are often kept away from school to work in the fields or to provide child care for younger children. In an interview study of elementary, middle, and high school migrant students, the students were asked about their school attendance. About half the students reported missing school for reasons other than illness; these reasons included translating for their parents, taking care of younger siblings, and working in the fields (Martinez, Scott, et al. 1994, 339). When schools require a specific number of days of school attendance for students to progress to the next grade level or to accrue credits, attendance becomes a critical issue.

In addition to mobility, many migrant children and youth experience difficulty in school because at home they speak a language other than English. The vast majority of migrant families speak Spanish as their home language; these children have difficulty participating successfully in schools and classrooms where there is inadequate language support. In his account of his own childhood experience, Jiménez writes about the difficulties he experienced going to a school where only English was spoken.

> Miss Scalapino started speaking to the class and I did not understand a word she was saying. The more she spoke, the more anxious I became. By the end of the day, I was very tired of hearing Miss Scalapino talk because the sounds made no sense to me. I thought that perhaps by paying close attention, I would begin to understand, but I did not. I only got a headache, and that night, when I went to bed, I heard her voice in my head. (Jiménez 1997, 17–18)

A large proportion of migrant parents speak little English or no English at all, making communication with schools difficult at best, and nonexistent at worst. In many cases, migrant children and youth have the responsibility of translating for their parents when schools do try to communicate.

Migrant parents often are not actively involved in their children's education, at least not in the ways that U.S. schools expect, another critical factor that could impede the children's academic success. Migrant parents work long hours, often from dawn until dark. Because wages for migrant workers are so low, when work is available, they must work. They cannot take time from their workdays to participate in school activities. Further, many migrant parents do not speak English and often have low levels of education themselves. They would not be able to assist their children with homework, even if the time were available to them. In their report on the involvement of migrant parents, Martinez and Velázquez quoted a migrant mother who wanted to help her children:

> With two of my children, I do very little because they go to higher grades . . . I don't have the education. What I do is . . . take them to the library so they can find information in books. . . . The one I do a little more with is the youngest, she is in fifth grade, so I sit with her and help her and I go over her homework. (Martinez and Velázquez 2000, 1)

And often the activities schools expect parents to participate in are offered in English only, excluding parents who do not speak English.

Another factor in parental involvement is the difference in expectations between schools in the United States and those in Mexico. Teachers from the United States who have participated in teacher exchanges with teachers from Mexico observed that "the limited roles parents have in Mexico's schools and in the decision-making process; parents allow teachers to make decisions about their children's schooling" that in the United States are more typically made by parents (Southwest Educational Development Laboratory 2000, 7). Parents who are accustomed to the cultural context of schools in Mexico may not understand the role that U.S. schools expect of them.

Social isolation is an additional factor that affects the educational success of migrant children and youth. Because they move often, these children and youth often do not have opportunities to form the social relationships with other children and youth that form the basis for the feelings of belonging that research shows to be so crucial in students' staying in school until they complete high school. Migrant parents, for various reasons, are often reluctant to be involved in their children's formal schooling or to participate in the activities that schools organize for parents. Because of their frequent moves, migrant parents rarely become a part of a school's social system, and what is more critical, they are often not informed about the school's expectations for their children's learning. Even when efforts are made to inform and involve migrant parents, they may find it difficult to make sense of the information because their own school experiences were probably very different from their children's.

This social isolation is exacerbated by how migrants are often viewed in the communities to which they migrate. Few communities welcome migrant workers or their families, and many of the demographic factors and the logistics of migration that place children and youth at risk educationally also serve as barriers to inclusion within communities. The majority of migrant workers in the United States are not part of the cultural mainstream. Many of them are binational, migrating between Mexico and the United States and bringing with them a culture that has customs, norms, and expectations different from those of the middle class in the United States. This social and cultural isolation may also create discontinuity between the schools and home experiences of migrant children and youth; varying expectations between home and school for such basics as social behavior and interaction may be difficult for parents to understand and for children to navigate.

Another barrier to education that migrant children and youth face is that many of them also participate in farm labor. Data provided by the U.S. Census Bureau shows that 17 percent of hired farmworkers in 1996 were under twenty years old, compared to 6 percent of all wage and salary earners (Runyan 1998, 3). Martinez, Scott, Cranston-Gingras, and Platt found that 75 percent of the elementary, middle, and high school students they interviewed in a study of migrant children and youth were working or had worked in the fields at the time of their interviews; some of the interviewees who reported working were as young as six (Martinez, Scott, et al. 1994, 338, 339). Migrant children and youth who are part of the labor force participate in strenuous physical labor. It is difficult for children who are performing this hard physical labor in the fields to find the energy at the end of the day to study and complete school work, even when there are opportunities to do so.

Still another factor is limited access to health care. Migrant children, youth, and their parents not only have problems accessing the health care system but also risk the serious potential effects of exposure to "dangerous chemicals and pesticides, either directly or indirectly," as a result of working in agriculture (Leon 1996, 1). Exposure to these chemicals can result in high rates of serious illnesses and conditions, including cancer and having children who suffer from birth defects. In addition, because of the difficulty of the timely transfer of school and health records of migrant children and youth, many have had too few or inaccurately spaced immunizations, or even more immunizations than are necessary. Migrant children and youth who are disabled or in need of specialized health support often go without these services or have gaps in service because of delays in transferring records.

Any one of these factors could place children at risk of educational failure. For most migrant children, several of these factors are combined, with the result that many migrant children and youth do not graduate from high school, and few have the opportunity for postsecondary education.

WHERE ARE THE SCHOOLS THAT SERVE MIGRANT CHILDREN AND YOUTH?

There are migrant children and migrant education programs in all fifty states, the District of Columbia, and Puerto Rico. In the 1997–1998 school year, the latest for which summary data are available, the U.S. Department of Education reported that 752,689 migrant children and youth were identified as eligible for migrant education programs in the United States. This figure represents the number of migrant children aged three through twenty-one who, within three years of a qualifying move, resided in a state for one or more days between September 1,

1997 and August 31, 1998. During the same school year, 621,464 of these children and youth were served in regular term or summer term migrant education programs, with 297,676 served only in summer or intersession programs. A table of state-by-state eligibility and participation in migrant education is provided in Table 1.3. The information provided in the table for each state is an unduplicated count; that is, each child or youth is counted only once within a state. At the national level, the count is duplicated; that is, the national total represents the total of participation from all states, the District of Columbia, and Puerto Rico. Students who travel from state to state may have been counted in each state in which they were enrolled.

The number of migrant children and youth being served by the Migrant Education Program has been increasing. In their 1998 evaluation of summer migrant projects, Parsad, Heaviside, Williams, and Farris noted that there were 283,000 Migrant Education Program participants in the summer of 1998, "a 28 percent increase in summer term participation from the previous year" (Parsad et al. 2000, 3). At the same time, regular school year participation decreased. The 1998 evaluation speculated that the decrease could have been caused, at least in part, by changes in the U.S. Department of Education's changes in eligibility rules for the Migrant Education Program (Parsad et al. 2000, 3).

Planning for the educational success of migrant children, youths, and adults must address the factors that place migrants at risk of failure. This planning offers a challenge to educators. It is not enough to have traditional content knowledge and pedagogical knowledge. Educators must investigate and engage in nontraditional forms of instructional delivery. They must coordinate their programs across the traditional educational boundaries of school districts, states, and countries. They must communicate and collaborate with educators in other school districts, states, and countries. They must be advocates for students and their families, helping them to access the health and social services needed to break down those barriers to learning. Educators of migrant children, youth, and adults must be the "border crossers" envisioned by Henry Giroux (1992) who have high levels of cultural knowledge, who understand their students' lives, and who create the spaces within their classrooms where those lives are honored and included.

> We cannot learn unless we collectively engage our families and children in solving their own problems and allowing them the opportunity for action and reflection. If we can do this, we will reclaim our humanity and engage our learners in building or strengthening communities. (Chahin 1998, 120)

TABLE 1.3 State-by-State Participation in Migrant Education Programs, 1997–1998

	Migrant Children and Youth Identified as Eligible to Be Served	Migrant Children and Youth Served		Migrant Children and Youth Identified as Eligible to Be Served	Migrant Children and Youth Served
Alabama	6,972	6,541	Nebraska	10,844	7,784
Alaska	13,125	5,531	Nevada	781	613
Arizona	18,173	18,173	New Jersey	3,115	3,245
Arkansas	14,965	11,059	New Hampshire	177	195
California	210,220	157,304	New Mexico	3,161	3,066
Colorado	13,029	13,633	New York	11,303	9,907
Connecticut	5,347	4,745	North Carolina	13,885	12,768
Delaware	573	232	North Dakota	982	785
District of Columbia	651	605	Ohio	5,357	3,800
Florida	52,941	35,937	Oklahoma	5,948	2,376
Georgia	14,973	16,097	Oregon	26,319	26,319
Idaho	10,780	10,780	Pennsylvania	12,549	13,476
Illinois	3,520	2,527	Puerto Rico	14,837	15,058
Indiana	7,149	8,073	Rhode Island	169	169
Iowa	4,025	2,011	South Carolina	1,776	1,093
Kansas	20,817	10, 591	South Dakota	2,252	920
Kentucky	25,038	25,038	Tennessee	1,174	759
Louisiana	6,041	5,255	Texas	116,912	123,437
Maine	9,838	6,211	Utah	2,793	2,505
Maryland	1,010	759	Virginia	1,933	1,933
Massachusetts	4,621	4,812	Vermont	1,265	1,185
Michigan	18,446	15,392	Washington	32,813	15,920
Minnesota	7,820	3,922	West Virginia	281	281
Mississippi	3,269	3,078	Wyoming	438	487
Missouri	4,730	3,113	Wisconsin	1,814	583
Montana	1,313	1,381			

SOURCE: *Title I Migrant Education State Performance Reports,* 1997–98, Office of Migrant Education, United States Department of Education.

REFERENCES

Andrade de Herrera, V. "Education in Mexico: Historical and Contemporary Educational Systems." In *Children of la Frontera: Binational Efforts to Serve Mexican Migrant and Immigrant Students,* edited by J. L. Flores, 25–60. Charleston, WV: Clearinghouse on Rural Education and Small Schools, 1996.

Chahin, J. "Mis Padres: What They Shared." *Educational Horizons* 76, no. 3 (1998): 120–121.

Chavkin, N. F. "Involving Migrant Families in Their Children's Education." In *Children of la Frontera: Binational Efforts to Serve Mexican Migrant and Immigrant Students,* edited by J. L. Flores, 325–340. Charleston, WV: Clearinghouse on Rural Education and Small Schools, 1996.

Davis, S. "Child Labor in Agriculture." *ERIC Digest* (report no. RC020945). Charleston, WV: Clearinghouse on Rural Education and Small Schools, 1997. (ERIC Document Reproduction Service No. ED 405159)

Elvia. "Detasseling." *Estupendas.* Newsletter of the ★Estrella Project (2000): 16.

Giroux, H. A. *Border Crossings: Cultural Workers and the Politics of Education.* New York: Routledge, 1992.

Jiménez, F. *The Circuit: Stories from the Life of a Migrant Child.* Albuquerque, NM: Univeristy of New Mexico Press, 1997.

Kindler, A. L. "Education of Migrant Children in the United States." *Directions in Language & Education* 1, no. 8 (1995): 1–11.

Leon, E. *The Health Condition of Migrant Farm Workers.* Lansing, MI: Michigan State Department of Education, 1996. (ERIC Document Reproduction Service No. ED 406074)

Macías, J. "The Social Nature of Instruction in a Mexican School: Implications for U.S. Classroom Practice." *The Journal of Educational Issues of Language Minority Students* 10 (spring 1992): 13–25.

Martin, P. L. "Migrant Farmworkers and Their Children." In *Children of la Frontera: Binational Efforts to Serve Mexican Migrant and Immigrant Students,* edited by J. L. Flores, 19–23. Charleston, WV: Clearinghouse on Rural Education and Small Schools, 1996.

Martinez, Y. G., J. Scott, Jr., A. Cranston-Gingras, and J. S. Platt. "Voices from the Fields: Interviews with Students from Migrant Farmworker Families." *The Journal of Educational Issues of Language Minority Students* 14 (1994): 333–347.

Martinez, Y. G., and J. A. Velázquez. "Involving Migrant Families in Education." *ERIC Digest* (report no. EDO-RC-00-4). Charleston, WV: Clearinghouse on Rural Education and Small Schools, 2000.

National Agricultural Statistics Service. *Farm Labor Report* (November). Washington, DC: U.S. Department of Agriculture, 2000.

Parsad, B., S. Heaviside, C. Williams, and E. Farris. *Title I Migrant Education Program Summer Term Projects, 1998.* Washington, DC: U.S. Department of Education Office of Educational Research and Improvement, 2000.

Rios, J. L. "Working in La Fresa." In *Voices from the Fields,* edited by S. B. Atkin, 10–17. Boston: Little, Brown and Company, 1993.

Romo, H. D. "The Newest 'Outsiders': Educating Mexican Migrant and Immigrant Youth." In *Children of la Frontera: Binational Efforts to Serve Mexican Migrant and Immigrant Students, edited by J. L. Flores, 61–91. Charleston, WV: Clearinghouse on Rural Education and Small Schools, 1996.

Rothenberg, D. *With These Hands: The Hidden World of Migrant Farmworkers Today.* Berkeley, CA: University of California Press, 1998.

Runyan, J. L. *Profile of Hired Farmworkers, 1996 Annual Averages* (Agricultural Economic Report No. 762). Washington, DC: U. S. Department of Agriculture, Economic Research Service, Food and Rural Economics Division, 1998.

Schlosser, E. "In the Strawberry Fields." *The Atlantic Monthly* 276, no. 5 (1995): 80–108.

Southwest Educational Development Laboratory. "Critical Features of Exchanges." *Educator Exchange Resource Guide,* 2000. Available: http://www.sedl.org/pubs/lco3/3.html

Takaki, R. *A Different Mirror: A History of Multicultural America.* Boston: Little, Brown and Company, 1993.

U.S. Department of Labor. *Findings from the National Agricultural Workers Survey (NAWS) 1997–1998: A Demographic and Employment Profile of United States Farmworkers.* Washington, DC: U.S. Department of Labor, Office of the Assistant Secretary for Policy, Office of Program Economics, 2000.

U.S. General Accounting Office. *Migrant Children: Education and HHS Need to Improve the Exchange of Participant Information* (Report to Congress). Washington, DC: U.S. General Accounting Office, 1999.

Valle, I. *Fields of Toil: A Migrant Family's Journey.* Pullman, WA: Washington State University Press, 1994.

NOTE

1. Julio Gaona is a young man whose family migrates from Texas to Oklahoma, Idaho, Utah, Oregon, and Washington. He is a student in the Corpus Christi Migrant Program. He wrote this poem about his experiences as a migrant and his hopes and dreams for the future. For this poem, Julio won first prize in the poetry division of the Eighth Annual Richard A. Bove Migrant Students' Poets and Writers Festival (2001). It is used here with his permission.

Chapter Two

Chapter Two

❧ Chronology

1950s   An interstate pilot migrant program is begun by the National Council on Agricultural Life and Labor and the Rural Education Association of the National Education Association.

1960   Edward R. Murrow's documentary, *Harvest of Shame,* is aired on Thanksgiving Day. The documentary makes public the conditions under which migrants live and work and initiates a public dialogue about migrant farmworkers and their living and working conditions.

Congress passes the Economic Opportunity Act, which allocates funding for migrant education. This is the first legislation at the federal level that specifically addresses education for migrant children and youth.

1962   Congress passes the Migrant Health Act, which provides support for clinics serving the special health needs of agricultural workers.

1965   The passage of the Elementary and Secondary Schools Act (Public Law 89–10) provides federal funding and guidance for supplemental compensatory education programs for children and youth in poverty.

The Higher Education Act (HEA), Section 418A, Public Law 89–329, provides for the High School Equivalency Program (HEP) and the College Assistance Migrant Program (CAMP) to help migrant youth complete high school and prepare to enter and be successful in postsecondary education.

The Head Start program is created to promote school readiness among children in poverty.

1966   Congress amends Title I of the Elementary and Secondary Schools Act to add special provisions for the education of migrant children and youth (Public Law 89–750). Funding is allocated specifically for migrant education, but the U.S. Office of Education is inadequately staffed to provide guidance to states in planning and administering migrant education programs.

The U.S. Department of Health, Education, and Welfare initiates the Migrant Health Center program to provide access to health care services for migrant workers and their families.

1967   The Elementary and Secondary Education Amendments (ESEA) of 1967, Public Law 90–247, inserts a new Title VII, the Bilingual Education Program, into the Elementary and Secondary Education Act. Title VII institutes federal government support for "children of limited English-speaking ability" between the ages of three and eighteen in the form of grants to state education agencies for bilingual education programs. Public Law 90–247 also provides for preservice training and inservice education to teachers, teacher aides, counselors, and other bilingual education program personnel.

The "Five Year Amendment" included in Public Law 90–247 allows states to serve children in migrant education programs for five years after they have stopped migrating. This provision leads to distinguishing between currently migrating students and formerly migrating students in program planning and in providing educational services.

The U.S. Department of Labor begins funding HEP (High School Equivalency Program) and CAMP (College Assistance Migrant Program).

The Bilingual Education Act is passed. This legislation encourages local school districts to research and implement instruction in students' first languages. Most states follow the lead of the federal government by enacting legislation that provides for bilingual education in the schools in those states.

1968   The first director of migrant education at the federal level, Vidal A. Rivera, Jr., is appointed.

1969   The Migrant Student Record Transfer System (MSRTS) begins. This nationwide system is intended to receive, maintain, and transmit the education and health records of migrant children as they travel from school to school. The system is also designed to provide aggregate data about eligible migrant students for use in planning at the state and federal levels.

      The U.S. Department of Health and Human Services extends the Head Start program to include provisions for a Migrant Head Start program.

1974   In *Lau v. Nichols,* the right of children to education in their first languages is upheld. The U.S. Supreme Court rules that a school district's failure to provide instruction in students' primary languages denies those students access to a public education.

      The Court of Appeals decision in *Casteñeda v. Pickard* (5th Cir. 1981), establishes a legal standard for meeting the needs of students whose first language was not English.

      Public Law 93–380, the Elementary and Secondary Education Amendments, extends the provisions of the Elementary and Secondary Education Act to 1978. The Amendments include the Equal Educational Opportunity Act, which establishes an Office of Bilingual Education in the U.S. Office of Education. They also initiate a series of activities related to bilingual education. These include establishing a National Advisory Council on bilingual education, directing the National Institute of Education to conduct research on bilingual education, providing grants for research and demonstration projects in bilingual education, and allocating funds for contracting with state education agencies to develop leadership in bilingual education. Title VII of the Amendments also appropriates funds for bilingual vocational education.

1975   The U.S. Department of Health, Education, and Welfare issues the *Lau* Remedies, a set of specific requirements for

1975, *cont.*	the provision of bilingual education for language minority students.

1976   In Public Law 94–482, the Education Amendments, Congress appropriates funding for grants to and contracts with state and local education agencies and other institutions for bilingual vocational training programs.

California is one of the first states to enact legislation that establishes a comprehensive bilingual education program. The Chacon-Moscone Bilingual-Bicultural Education Act responds to the *Lau v. Nichols* Supreme Court decision and the *Lau* Remedies.

1978   The Portable Assisted Study Sequence (PASS) originates in California. The purpose of the PASS program is to provide the opportunity for high school students to continue to accrue credits toward graduation through self-directed study as they migrate from state to state and from one school system to another.

In Public Law 95–561, Congress extends funding for the Elementary and Secondary Education Act for five years, through 1983.

1979   The Department of Education Organization Act (Public Law 96–88) is signed into law, creating a separate Department of Education. The U.S. Department of Health, Education, and Welfare becomes the U.S. Department of Health and Human Services.

1980   The Association of Mexican American Educators meets for the first time in Mexico City. This meeting is the formal beginning of collaboration between teachers and schools in Mexico and the United States. This collaboration is intended to support students who migrate between schools in the United States and Mexico. The Office of International Relations in the Mexican Ministry of Education administers these programs.

1982   In the U.S. Supreme Court *Plyer vs. Doe* decision, reversing a decision from a Texas court, the Court rules that undocumented children are entitled to public education, as well as bilingual education, Chapter 1 (federally funded compensatory education) programs, Head Start, free and reduced-cost lunches, and other programs necessary for their success in school.

The Binational Project between California and Michoacàn begins. This project supports research that documents the issues and problems faced by children and youth who migrate back and forth across the U.S.-Mexican border, resulting (in 1986) in a Binational Transfer Document that simplifies the transfer of students between schools in Mexico and several states in the United States.

1988   Congress passes the Augustus F. Hawkins-Robert T. Stafford Elementary and Secondary School Improvement Act of 1988 (Public Law 100–297). This legislation amends Chapter 1 of Title I of the Elementary and Secondary Schools Act to focus on accountability, program improvement, direct participation of parents in educational programs funded under the legislation, schoolwide projects, and increased coordination between Chapter 1 and other services. The provision for coordination includes that between regular Chapter 1 programs and Chapter 1 Migrant programs.

The Adult Education Act, Section 372 of Public Law 100–297, establishes the National Center for ESL (English as a Second Language) Literacy Education (NCLE). The center is funded by English Literacy Grants authorized under Public Law 100–297.

1990   Mexican president Carlos Salinas establishes the Program for Mexican Communities Abroad. This program is intended to link communities in the United States whose heritage is predominantly Mexican with communities in Mexico. The program supports exchanges of teachers between these communities, and provides educational coursework and educational materials to schools in the U.S. communities involved.

A Memorandum of Agreement is signed by U.S. Secretary of Education Lauro Cavazos and Mexican Secretary of Education Manuel Bartlett-Diaz to establish educational ties be-

1990, *cont.*	tween the two countries. The agreement as originally signed extends through 1991 and includes a provision for the agreement to be renewed automatically for two additional years with each renewal.

The National Association of State Directors of Migrant Education appoints a committee to examine ways to improve migrant education. This committee later becomes the Migrant Education Goals Task Force.

1991   The National Literacy Act (Public Law 102–103) amends the Adult Education Act, providing for state literacy resource centers, workplace literacy grants, English literacy grants, and the Education Program for Commercial Drivers.

1992   The Higher Education Act is reauthorized (Public Law 102–325) and extends the provisions for HEP and CAMP through 1997.

The Migrant Education Goals Task Force issues a report that responds, from the perspective of migrant education, to the National Education Goals, its purpose being to initiate a discussion at the national level about what quality education means for migrant students.

1994   Congress reauthorizes Title I of the Elementary and Secondary Schools Act with the passage of the Improving America's Schools Act (Public Law 103–382). This legislation provides for the Migrant Education Program to be included as a part of Title I schoolwide programs. It also reduces the eligibility for migrant education programs from six years to three, removing about 200,000 children who were previously eligible for services, but adding the eligibility of workers and their spouses through age twenty-one. The statute also begins the phase-out of MSRTS and mandates that a new means of counting eligible students be developed, as well as new means of transferring student records.

Proposition 187 is passed by California voters. This controversial proposition prohibits public social services, including health care and education, to undocumented individuals. It also mandates that school personnel report undocumented children and youth to the Immigration and Naturalization Service.

In response to the Goals 2000 Educate America Act, which calls for the development of challenging academic standards at the national and state levels, the National Association of State Directors of Migrant Education publishes Opportunity-to-Learn Standards for migrant students.

1996 The New Generation System (NGS) begins operation. This new system, a collaborative effort among twenty-nine states, is developing an Internet-based format for transfer of migrant student records.

The Immigration Act (Public Law 104–51) is signed into law. This legislation reserves the right to enact immigration law and to set immigration policy to the federal government, and prohibits states from enacting immigration law.

1997 The Federal District Court in Los Angeles rules that all provisions of Proposition 187 are unconstitutional; the ruling is based on the 1996 Immigration Act that prohibits state regulation of immigration.

1998 California voters pass Proposition 297, which restricts the use of students' first languages (if they are not English) for instruction, instead requiring that schools provide structured English immersion for students whose first language is not English. Students may participate in the structured English immersion for only one year. Parents may seek waivers for their children to be exempt from participating in the structured English immersion classrooms.

The Workforce Investment Act (Public Law 105–220), which includes the Adult Education and Family Literacy Act, is enacted. This legislation brings together federal employment, adult education, and vocational rehabilitation programs to create an integrated, one-stop system of workforce investment and education activities for adults and youth.

1999 The current authorization for the ESEA, 1994 Improving America's Schools Act, is scheduled to expire this year. Con-

1999,   gress and the White House begin the work of reauthorization
cont.   but do not finish.

2000   Reauthorization work on ESEA begins again but is still not
        completed.

2001   The Migrant Education Program celebrates its thirty-fifth
        birthday.

        A new reauthoriztion of the Elementary and Secondary Edu-
        cation Act is scheduled to be enacted by Congress.

Chapter Three

✏ Migrant Education in the United States: A Historical Perspective

Although migrant workers have lived in the United States throughout our history, little public attention was directed toward them, their working and living conditions, or their education until the airing of Edward R. Murrow's classic documentary, *Harvest of Shame,* on Thanksgiving Day, 1960. That documentary raised public awareness about what had been a largely invisible population, and initiated a public dialogue about the issues migrant workers and their families face. Out of that dialogue came the impetus for efforts by the federal government that addressed health care, working and living conditions, and the education of migrant children, youth, and adults. In 1964, the Economic Opportunity Act was enacted. This legislation allocated federal funding for programs that specifically addressed the unique educational needs of migrant students. This chapter will trace the development of migrant education in the United States, from its beginnings in local efforts for migrant education and early interstate programs to the present.

EARLY EFFORTS AT MIGRANT EDUCATION

Before 1964, migrant education efforts were sporadic, "initiated by private organizations and . . . directed toward only a few children" (National Committee on the Education of Migrant Children 1971, iii). Most of these initiatives were in the form of local programs, often sponsored and developed by social service or philanthropic agencies rather than by schools or school districts, that did little to address the educational discontinuity migrant children and youth face. As early as the 1950s, the need for a program that did address this discontinuity was recognized. In the 1950s, an interstate pilot migrant education program was researched and initiated by the National Council on Agricultural Life and Labor (NCALL) and the Rural Education Association (REA) of the National Education Association (NEA). According to Cassandra Stockburger, the executive director of the National Committee for the Education of Migrant Children, the NEA published reports of this project in 1954 and 1960. These reports documented the educational discontinuity that migrant children faced, as well as their sporadic school attendance. Shirley E. Greene, the author of the 1954 report, described the issue as it affected school attendance: "Less than 43 percent of migrant children received 150 days of schools, while 14.8 percent got less than 120 days. After age fifteen, attendance dropped to less than 50 days of school per year. Less than one in five of those enrolled at all reported attending as many as 150 days" (Stockburger 1980, 11).

The reports also concluded that teachers were unprepared to meet the needs of migrant students; they were particularly lacking the diagnostic skills required to determine the academic needs of migrating children and to place them appropriately in educational programs when they arrived in new schools (Stockburger 1980, 9–11).

There are accounts of local programs for migrant students in place prior to the federal legislation. Many of these programs were summer programs. James McGeehan describes a summer migrant program that began in 1964:

> The Chester County Migrant Summer School was organized by the
> Chester County Board of School Directors in 1964 and opened its doors
> for the first time that summer. . . . The enrollment for the 1964 term was
> seventeen children of migrant workers, all of them American Negroes
> whose home base was South Carolina and Florida. A professional staff
> of three teachers and one teaching principal was hired in addition to a
> dietitian and a kitchen helper. Supplies were purchased and salaries
> paid from monies allocated by the Commonwealth [of Pennsylvania].
> The children of the migrant school were fed two meals a day: breakfast
> and lunch. Furthermore, a team consisting of an MD and a nurse came
> to the school and examined the children, inoculating those who
> needed it. A social worker had visited the parents in the camp to deter
> mine who needed the vaccinations.
>
> The curriculum that first year consisted of academic subjects in the
> morning and Arts and Crafts and Physical Education in the afternoon.
> Much emphasis was placed on the development of social and sanitary
> skills, i.e., washing hands, brushing teeth, clean clothes and the use of
> "please," "thank you," "excuse me." It was felt at the end of the four-
> week term that much progress had been made in this area. The aca
> demic progress was difficult to measure due to the shortness of the pe
> riod. (McGeehan 1969, 119)

The U.S. Office of Education (part of the U.S. Department of Health, Education, and Welfare at that time) did designate a staff member to answer questions and deal with issues related to migrant education several years before the 1966 amendment. But no substantial funds were available to develop migrant education programs before the 1966 amendment (National Committee on the Education of Migrant Children 1971, 5).

In 1964, educators from across the country met at the first National Conference of Migrant Education in St. Louis, Missouri, to identify and address issues related to educating migrant children. Specifically, the conference addressed (1) the methodology and basic content of an educational program that would meet the needs of migrant children; (2) the coordination of available community services; and (3) the resources available to states for migrant education through federal and state programs (Stockburger 1980, 11). This first national conference identified the issue of educational discontinuity as critical to migrant education and set the agenda for migrant education at the federal government level that continues to this day.

With the passage of the Economic Opportunity Act (EOA) in 1960, a grant was awarded under Title III-B of the EOA to the National Committee for the Education of Migrant Children (NCEMC) to develop a plan that would address the educational discontinuity experienced by migrant children as the most pressing issue in their education. According to Stockburger, then director of the NCEMC, "this appears to be the first time that the term continuity was seriously applied to program development for migrant children" (Stockburger 1980, 12). The NCEMC convened a series of meetings and workgroups to develop recommendations for a migrant education program. These recommendations addressed curriculum and textbooks; the establishment of a clearinghouse of information on migrant children, their demographics and needs, and information about appropriate curriculum and teaching materials and strategies, professional development for school personnel; strategies for use and communication of health and education records; and the provision of a mobile team that would move with children and help to provide a continuity of services to migrant children and families. The NCEMC further recommended the inclusion of day care and the development of a demonstration project to explore the issues of educational continuity (Stockburger 1980, 12–13).

According to Stockburger, the recommendations led to a proposal for the development of a migrant education program. The proposal was submitted to the Office of Economic Opportunity (OEO) in 1965. The NCEMC-proposed migrant education program would include a communications network; a day care program that would serve as a channel of communication as well as coordinate education, day care, and health services; and a technical assistance laboratory for migrant education. "Although this comprehensive proposal was requested by OEO, OEO did not fund it, apparently because of a change in leadership which placed a lesser priority on services to children" (Stockburger 1980, 14). At a 1968 meeting of Title I ESEA Migrant Coordinators, a spokesperson for the OEO confirmed the reordering of priorities and explained that the migrant education program proposal had not been funded because the OEO's funds were limited, requiring setting the priority for serving adults and families. According to that spokesperson, "there [were] between 4.5 and 9 million people who [fell] within the category which Title III-B [sought] to serve. OEO therefore [had] roughly $4 per person per annum to get these farm workers out of poverty" (Office of Education [DHEW] 1969, 18).

MIGRANT EDUCATION SINCE THE 1966 MIGRANT EDUCATION AMENDMENT

In 1965, Public Law 89–10, the Elementary and Secondary Education Act (ESEA) was enacted. Title I of the ESEA, Public Law 89–10, initiated federal government involvement in and funding for supplemental compensatory education for children and youth in poverty. In 1966, the ESEA was amended (Public Law 89–750) to include special provisions and funding allocated for a migrant education program. This legislation was sponsored by William Ford, a congressman from Michigan, to address the unique educational needs of the children of migrant farmworkers, a group that had been overlooked in the 1965 ESEA.

It is important to understand that the funds provided for and programs authorized under the ESEA have always been intended to be supplemental. That is, they do not take the place of state and/or locally funded basic education programs. Rather, these compensatory education programs are intended to provide additional educational opportunities for children and youth in poverty.

Since it was first enacted in 1965, Title I of the ESEA has been reauthorized several times. Each of the reauthorizations has addressed concerns and issues raised in the evaluations of the previous reauthorizations. For example, a 1971 evaluation of the effectiveness of the original Migrant Amendment concluded that "the Migrant Amendment to Title I of the Elementary and Secondary Education Act has succeeded in mobilizing most State Education Agencies to develop services for migrant children. These efforts vary greatly in the degree of their commitment, competence and effectiveness. However, migrant children cannot yet count on finding programs geared to their needs in many communities which they enter" (National Committee on the Education of Migrant Children 1971, 115).

This evaluation made several recommendations that have been addressed as the legislation has been revised and reauthorized. Each reauthorization has also reflected trends and issues in education in the United States in general at the time of the reauthorization.

THE IDENTIFICATION OF MIGRANT CHILDREN AND YOUTH AND MIGRANT EDUCATION PROGRAM FUNDING

The largest challenges of the 1966 Migrant Education Program were the identification of migrant students and the allocation of funds in the form of grants to states. These issues were interrelated because funding was allocated to the states based on how many school-aged migrant children were in the states. In 1966, the U.S. Office of Education used data provided by the U.S. Department of Labor's Office of Farm Labor to determine the number of migrant children in the states. The National Committee on the Education of Migrant Children evaluation reported that the number of migrant children in each state was computed at 75 percent of the estimated monthly average (or "full-time equivalency") of adult migrants employed in that state during the most recent year for which U.S. Department of Labor estimates had been compiled (National Committee on the Education of Migrant Children 1971, 9).

This magic formula was based on an assumption in the absence of real data about the number of children and youth who traveled with adult migrants. Compiling employment statistics on migrant labor was confounded by the several factors endemic to migrant farm labor discussed in Chapter 1, not the least of which was the definition of migrant.

The definition of migrant is a particularly critical issue for migrant education programs. Funding in general for the Migrant Education Program and reallocation of funds through grants to states and local education agencies has historically been based on the number of migrant workers or the number of eligible migrant students in the United States and in each state and local school district. The definition of migrant is critical also because states and school districts must be able to determine who is eligible for migrant education services; eligibility for service should be consistent from state to state, school district to school district.

In guidance for implementing the 1966 amendment, the U.S. Office of Education defined a migrant child as one who had "moved with his family from one school district to another during the past year in order that a parent or other member of his immediate family might secure employment in agriculture or in related food processing" (National Committee on the Education of Migrant Children 1971, 9–10). The definition included no guidance in defining "agriculture or . . . related food processing," and states' definitions varied widely.

According to the 1971 evaluation of the Migrant Education Program conducted by the National Committee on Migrant Education, the definition was explicitly interpreted in some states by the state education departments; in other states, the interpretation of the definition was left up to local education agencies. In Florida, a migrant program director explained how families were identified as being eligible for the migrant education program, and mentioned the involvement of the state education department: "The largest number of parents work[ed] in the citrus groves. A few [were] in related occupations, such a driving trucks or processing citrus concentrate. The State Education Department disallowed the inclusion of peripheral occupations such as workers in phosphate mines, even though phosphate is used a fertilizer in the groves" (National Committee on the Education of Migrant Children 1971, 10).

By contrast, in a New York state school district, the migrant education project coordinator explained that children were served in the migrant program even if their parents were as peripherally involved in agriculture as manufacturing shovels (National Committee on the Education of Migrant Children 1971, 10). This variation in definition resulted in wide discrepancy in determining who was eligible for service from state to state and, in some cases, from school district to school district.

Beginning in 1967, the U.S. Office of Education gained an additional source of information about the number of migrant children. As part of their applications for federal migrant education funds, state education agencies (SEAs) filed estimates of the number of school-aged migrant children to be served in migrant education programs in their states. The National Committee on the Education of Migrant Children found great disparity between the data provided by the U.S. Department of Labor and that provided by the SEAs. "For example, for fiscal year 1969, state education agencies estimated a total of 208,872 children 'to be served,' while the 'magic formula' [75 percent of adult migrant farmworkers] yielded a 'full-time equivalency' of 157,153" (National Committee on the Education of Migrant Children 1971, 9).

With each subsequent reauthorization, the language of the legislation has become more carefully delineated to help ensure service to migrant students that is consistent among states and school districts across the country. In Public Law 103–382, the Improving America's Schools Act (1994), the latest reauthorization of the Elementary and Secondary Schools Act, the U.S. Department of Education provides a specific definition of migrant and parameters for applying that definition.

For the purposes of determining eligibility for the migrant education programs (MEP), Public Law 103–382 defines "qualifying employment" as "any temporary or seasonal agricultural or fishing work . . . if it constitutes a principal means of livelihood" (U.S. Department of Education 1996a, 1).

In addition, the department includes detailed definitions of the specific tasks that are considered agricultural or fishing work, including definitions of crop production and processing, cultivation and harvesting, and fish farms, along with examples of these categories (U.S. Department of Education 1996a, 2, 3).

Further, the document provides guidance in how to apply the definitions to determine children and youth who may be served in migrant education programs. According to the statute, a child is eligible for MEP services if he or she

1. Is younger than twenty-two (and has not graduated from high school or does not hold a high school equivalency certificate), *but,* if the child is too young to attend school-sponsored educational programs, is old enough to benefit from an organized instructional program
2. Is a migrant agricultural worker or a migrant fisher (as defined in Section 1309 of the statute) or has a parent, spouse, or guardian who is a migrant agricultural worker or a migrant fisher
3. Performs, or has a parent, spouse, or guardian who performs, qualifying agricultural or fishing employment as a principal means of livelihood
4. Has moved within the preceding thirty-six months to obtain, or to accompany or join a parent, spouse, or guardian to obtain, temporary or seasonal employment in agricultural or fishing work
5. Has moved from one school district, or
6. In a state that is comprised of a single school district, has moved from one administrative area to another within such district, or
7. Resides in a school district of more than 15,000 square miles, and migrates a distance of twenty miles or more to a tempo-

rary residence to engage in a fishing activity (this provision
currently applies only to Alaska) (U.S. Department of
Education 1996a)

Section 1309 of the statute further defines agricultural activity as "any
activity directly related to the production or processing of crops, dairy
production, poultry, or livestock for initial commercial sale or personal
subsistence" (34 CFR 200.40(a)(1)). The regulatory guidance provides
additional definitions and examples to assist states and school districts
in identifying eligible migrant children and youth. The statute requires
states to record a Certificate of Eligibility for each student identified in
the state as eligible. The Certificate of Eligibility documents the basis on
which the student has been identified as migrant and therefore eligible
for service in the migrant education program. A sample Certificate of Eligibility is shown in Table 3.1.

Identification and recruitment of migrant students is, according
to the regulatory guidance, "a cornerstone" of the Migrant Education
Program, and critical because

- ➬ The children who are most in need of program services are
  often those who are the most difficult to find.
- ➬ Many migrant children would not fully benefit from school,
  and in some cases, would not attend school at all, if the
  SEAs did not identify and recruit them into the MEP. (This is
  particularly true of the most mobile migrant children who
  may be more difficult to identify than those who have set-
  tled within a community.)
- ➬ Children cannot receive MEP services without a record of
  eligibility. (U.S. Department of Education 1996a, 1)

The Preliminary Guidance includes various strategies for identifying
migrant children. The guidance suggests that states

- ➬ Identify and map the locations of agricultural and commercial fishing area. The U.S. Departments of Agriculture,
  Labor, and Commerce, and the State Office of Employment
  Security, can assist in many cases. Regional and local MEP
  staff may wish to contact individual growers and other agricultural and fishing employers.
- ➬ Obtain and maintain current information on the state's agricultural and fishing activities, and determine for each (1)
  areas of the state in which concentrations of migratory labor

exist; and (2) peak employment periods. Ensure that recruitment staff are deployed in areas where concentrations of migrants are likely to reside.

•• Coordinate with officials who administer the Women, Infants and Children (WIC), Migrant Health, Migrant Labor, Migrant Head Start, Community Service Block Grant programs, and other programs about the locations of migrant workers and families whom those programs serve. In some locations recruiters canvas local churches, ESL classes, farmworker unions, legal aid agencies, and local businesses like Laundromats, shopping malls, grocery stores, movie theaters, and restaurants to find migrant families.

•• Locate and maintain current lists of migrant housing in each area of the state. State and federal Departments of Health (or Health and Human Services) and Labor may have lists of migrant camps.

•• Evaluate periodically the effectiveness of the state's identification efforts, and revise procedures as necessary. (U.S. Department of Education 1996a, 2)

Successful identification and recruitment of migrant children and youth depends on having in place an identification and recruitment plan at the state and local levels. The success of these efforts also depends in part on the qualifications of the persons responsible for conducting the interviews that provide information upon which to determine the eligibility of children and youth for migrant education programs. The guidance provided by the U.S. Department of Education also suggests qualifications for recruiters. These qualifications include knowledge of

> basic MEP eligibility requirements; local agricultural and fishing production and processing sites; languages spoken by migratory workers; cycles of seasonal employment and temporary employment; local growers and fishing companies; local roads and locations of places where migrants typically live; MEP services offered by the local operating agency; the workings of the local school system; and other agencies that can provide services to migratory workers and their families, such as Migrant Health, Migrant Labor, WIC, and Migrant Head Start. (U.S. Department of Education 1996a, 2)

Many states, local agencies, and local school districts have developed identification and recruitment plans that involve networking and col-

TABLE 3.1. Sample Certificate of Eligibility

SAMPLE CERTIFICATE OF ELIGIBILITY

FAMILY DATA

1. Name and address of (1) persons responsible for the child OR (2) self-eligible youth

2. Name(s) of (1) the person from whom the information was obtained, and (2) the person who was informed of the Family Educational Rights and Privacy Act and told that the children's records may be sent to other schools where the child intends to enroll:

Legal parent (if not named above):

CHILD DATA

3. Name of child/youth

4. Sex

5. Birthdate

ELIGIBILITY DATA—The children listed moved

6. From (school, district, city, state, country)

7. To (school or school district)

8. Arriving (qualifying arrival date)

9. The child(ren) moved { } with, { } to join, OR { } on his/her own

10. { } Parent, { } Guardian, { } Spouse, or Self Name:

11. To enable that person to obtain or seek: { } Temporary, { } Seasonal, AND { } Agricultural { } Fishing employment Qualifying Activity:

12. Residency Date

13. Identify and describe other work (in addition to agricultural or fishing work), IF ANY, in which household members are engaged

14. Comments

15. Based on the interview, the interviewer has determined that the qualifying work is an important part of providing a living for the worker and his or her family.

Reviewer
Initials:
Date:

Interviewer: Date:

source: Preliminary Guidance for Migrant Education Program, Title I, Part C Public Law 103-382. Available: http://www.ed.gov/offices/OESE/MEP /PrelimGuide/certif.html.

laboration with other states and with employers and other agencies within their states. Some of the most innovative and successful identification and recruitment plans are described in subsequent chapters.

By adding a further amendment to the 1966 Migrant Education Amendment, the U.S. Office of Education did recognize in 1968 that the effects of migration on students' education were long term and were not remedied simply by settling out. This amendment, called the Five Year Amendment, provided for the Migrant Education Program to serve not only currently migrating students but also formerly migrating students. Regulatory guidance indicated that students should be included in the migrant program for five years after the last qualifying migration. But according to the 1971 evaluation, there was little consistency among state departments of education or local school districts in serving children who were formerly migrant.

> Eight states (California, Idaho, Montana, Nebraska, New Mexico, South Carolina, Utah, and Virginia) reported serving current migrants only during both regular and summer sessions. Two other states (Florida and Texas) reported serving only current migrants during the school year, with small numbers of "five-year" migrants during the summer. However, in six states (Illinois, Massachusetts, Missouri, New Jersey, Oklahoma, and Washington), half or more of all migrant children served during both sessions were reported as "five-year" migrants, and two states (Mississippi and Vermont) reported all children served as five-year migrants. (National Committee on the Education of Migrant Children 1971, 10–11)

Subsequent reauthorizations of the Migrant Education Program continue to recognize that the effects of migration can be long term. Eligibility for migrant education services was extended from five years after settling out to six years. The latest reauthorization (1994) limits this extended service to three years after what is considered a qualifying move; the intent is to focus funding and the resultant migrant education programs on children and youth who move most frequently, and on those children and youth most at risk of failing to meet state learning standards.

The issue of definition was, and is still, a critical one. The definition is the basis for identification of migrant children and youth not only for purposes of allocation of funding but also for the recruitment of students for migrant education programs, as well as program development and implementation. But the definition is only the beginning. Identification and recruitment of eligible migrant children and youth is even more critical. According to DiCerbo, "not all migrant students participate in the national MEP [Migrant Education Program]. Identification is inconsistent, with an undetermined number of migrant students never identified for special instruction" (DiCerbo 2001, 8).

Funding for the Migrant Education Program has historically come from the federal government, although some programs have been funded locally, and a few states, Virginia among them, currently provide some funding at the state level. In fiscal year 1967, the first year that funding was provided from Title I of the Elementary and Secondary Education Act for migrant education, $9.7 million was allocated, with $9.5 million of those funds being allocated in the form of grants to state departments of education. Funding for the Migrant Education Program increased significantly in the second year of the program; fiscal 1968 allocations to states totaled $37.7 million.

Funding has continued to increase; the appropriation for the Migrant Education Program for fiscal year 2001 is set at $380 million. In addition to grants to states for operating school year, intersession, and summer migrant education programs, the appropriation also includes funding for coordination grants and interstate collaboration. The grants to states are based on the number of children and youth identified as being eligible for migrant education services in the states.

Dividing the amount that is spent in grants to states by the number of students served in the program results in an average amount of about $600 for each student served in the Migrant Education Program. Although the total amount of funding may seem significant, $600 per student seems to be very little to offset the educational barriers faced by migrant children and youth.

According to Illinois state director of migrant education, David Gutierrez, the Migrant Education Program has never been fully funded; that is, the amount of funding appropriated for the Migrant Education Program has not matched the program authorization. While there seems to be some disagreement among migrant educators on the level of underfunding, there is general agreement that the program has traditionally been seriously underfunded, and that a much higher level of funding would be required to meet the goals of the program and the educational needs of all the children, youth, and families eligible for service through the Migrant Education Program.

MEETING THE EDUCATIONAL NEEDS OF MIGRANT CHILDREN AND YOUTH

Once students are identified, the issue becomes one of designing programs and delivery systems that address the specific needs of migrant children and youth. The 1966 Migrant Education Amendment provided little guidance for planning programs. The 1971 evaluation of the Migrant Education Program found that the quality of educational plans, the curriculum of the projects, and the instruction in those projects varied greatly; the evaluation recommended that the U.S. Office of Education take a stronger role in assisting states and local projects in setting objectives and developing plans that "are built on specific assessment of the individual educational needs and interests of the migrant children served" (National Committee on the Education of Migrant Children 1971, 117).

In later reauthorizations, more regulation and guidance were provided for program planning. In the 1988 Augustus F. Hawkins-Robert T. Stafford Elementary and Secondary School Improvement Act (Public Law 100–297), school districts were required to show evidence of comprehensive assessment of student needs as the basis for program planning and service delivery. In response to the standards movement of the 1990s, the 1994 Improving America's Schools Act (Public Law 103–382) requires migrant education programs to help students meet the same high standards for academic performance set by the states for all children. The guidance also includes strong statements about a focus on teaching and learning.

Like other compensatory education programs provided for in the Elementary and Secondary Schools Act and its reauthorizations, the Migrant Education Program has changed from a program whose curriculum content and objectives were separate from regular school programs to a program intended to assist students in meeting the same standards set for the regular program. Regulatory guidance for the Improving America's Schools Act (1994) calls for schools and school districts to provide, in addition to services that are comparable to those provided for all other students in the school district, support services aimed at addressing the special needs of migrant students. These services include

- Advocacy and outreach activities for migrant children and families to help them gain access to other education, health, nutrition, and social services
- Professional development programs, including mentoring, for teachers and other program personnel
- Family literacy programs, including those developed under Even Start
- Integration of information technology into educational and related programs
- The transition of secondary school students to postsecondary education or employment (U.S. Department of Education 1996b, 1, 2)

A critical factor in student success is family support. The Migrant Education Program provides for the development of family support through such family literacy programs as the Migrant Even Start Program and a strong mandate for the development of parent involvement components for all migrant education programs. The Migrant Education Even Start Program, first funded in 1989, combines early childhood education with parenting education and adult education, and helps link families to other education, health care, and social services available within their communities.

Instruction to students in the Migrant Education Program is offered during regular term programs and summer term programs. During the 1997–1998 school year, 525,738 students were served in regular term programs, and 312, 415 students were served in summer term programs.

Historically, instruction was provided to students in the Migrant Education Program either in separate classrooms, in pull-out programs that removed students from their regular classrooms for a part of the school day, or in programs that were offered before or after school, extending the school day for these students. Many summer programs served Migrant Education Program students only. This segregation of migrant children was a result, at least in part, of the prohibition against the commingling of funds that was part of the Elementary and Secondary Education Act. States, school districts, and schools were required not only to account for the outcomes they set for programs funded under ESEA; they were also required to account for the funding spent on materials and services related specifically to the program for which the funds were designated. Those materials and resources were to be used only for students eligible to participate in that program. This segregation did little to address the social isolation migrant children and their families faced in the communities to which they migrated.

The latest reauthorization of the Migrant Education Program under the Improving America's Schools Act (1994) encourages schools to serve migrant students in schoolwide programs. These programs offer a seamless educational program for students; they address educational needs within the regular classroom and the regular instructional program of the school without segregating migrant students from other students in the school.

Schoolwide programs allow schools to use compensatory education funds to "upgrade a school's entire educational program, provided that federal funds taken as a whole supplement state and local funds that would otherwise be spent at the school" (Migrant Education Program 1995d, 1). In other words, schools with schoolwide programs are not required to operate a series of separate categorical programs; they are allowed to combine the federal funds they receive for categorical programs with other state and local funds to address the whole school program. Schoolwide programs have been used to lower class size, to provide in-class instructional support in the form of teacher assistants or paraprofessionals, to hire additional teachers to provide such specialized services as language support in classrooms, and so on. Schoolwide programs that include Migrant Education Program funds and serve eligible migrant children and youth must ensure that these programs address the specific educational needs of migrant students. The schools are expected to provide information about the progress of migrant students as part of their accountability.

Schoolwide programs were first authorized in 1988. At that time, schoolwide programs "allowed Title I, Part A funds to be used to enhance the overall education program of schools rather than to target supplemental services to Title I-eligible students in schools with a poverty rate of 75 percent or higher" (Siler et al. 1999a, 2). The Improving America's Schools Act (1994) reduced the poverty threshold for schoolwide programs incrementally from 75 to 50 percent. The 50 percent threshold has been in effect since the 1996–1997 school year. The Improving America's Schools Act also allows schools to combine funds from a variety of federal, state, and local programs as long as the intent and purpose of each of the separate programs are met in the schoolwide program. In combining Migrant Education Program funds, for example, schools are required to "consult with migrant parents or their representatives, address the needs of migrant children that result from the effects of their migrant lifestyle or are needed to permit migrant children to participate effectively in the school, and document that appropriate services have been provided to them (ESEA Section 1306(b)(3) and 34 CFR 200.8(c)(3))"(Siler et al. 1999a, 3).

The Improving America's Schools Act requires schoolwide programs to include the following components:

1. Comprehensive needs assessment of the entire school that is based on information on the performance of children in relation to the state content standards and the state student performance standards
2. Schoolwide reform strategies that address the needs of the students targeted by the programs that are included in the schoolwide program
3. Instruction by highly qualified professional staff
4. Professional development for teachers and aides, other school personnel, and parents
5. Strategies to increase parent involvement, such as family literacy services

6. Plans for assisting preschool children in the transition from early childhood programs, such as Head Start, Even Start, or a state-run preschool program, to local elementary school programs

7. Measures to include teachers in the decisions regarding the use of assessments to provide information on, and to improve, the performance of individual students and the overall instructional program

8. Activities to ensure that student who experience difficulty mastering any of the state standards will be provided with effective, timely assistance

In an evaluation of the effectiveness of schoolwide programs for migrant students mandated by Congress in the Improving America's Schools Act, Siler, Stolzberg, von Glatz, and Strang (1999) found that, in general, "schoolwide programs appear to be addressing the needs of migrant students. Migrants participate fully in the services provided by schoolwide programs and usually have access to an additional array of services provided by the district migrant education program" (Siler et al. 1999b, 1). The evaluators concluded with the caveat that teachers and other personnel in some schools did not know which children were eligible for Migrant Education Program services, and few, if any, accommodations had been made specifically for migrant children in assessment.

Migrant Education Program funds were combined with other funds to support the schoolwide programs in only about one-third of the schools included in the study. Researchers found that, among other reasons, "migrant program and district and school staff were hesitant to eliminate all categorical services for students in need because they were concerned that their needs might be overlooked" (Siler et al. 1999b, 3). Chapter 4 includes the description of a schoolwide program that serves migrant children. The program was recognized by the U.S. Department of Education as a model in addressing the needs of migrant children in a schoolwide program.

INTERSTATE AND INTRASTATE COORDINATION AND COLLABORATION

To "reduce the effects of educational disruption on migrant children in order to remove barriers to their educational achievement," the Migrant Education Program includes incentives in the form of grants for the development and implementation of coordination and collaborative activities between and among local school districts and states (Migrant Education Program 1995c, 1). This coordination and collaboration is intended to support the following types of strategies:

- ➡ Developing credit accrual and credit exchange programs
- ➡ Coordinating curriculum development
- ➡ Exchanging teachers and teaching materials
- ➡ Implementing dropout prevention programs
- ➡ Exchanging information on health screenings and health problems that interrupt the student's education
- ➡ Promoting the exchange of school records (Migrant Education Program 1995c, 1)

Examples of effective coordination and collaboration can be found in many migrant programs and activities. These include consortia of states focused on identification and recruitment of migrant children and youth, such as the Consortium Agreement, Identification and Recruitment (CAIR); efforts made between the Texas Migrant Program and several other states to coordinate curriculum with that of schools in Texas and to take the Texas Assessment of Academic Skills (TAAS) test off-site in other states; both interstate and binational teacher exchange programs; and the New Generation System (NGS) for exchanging student health and education records. Examples will be described more fully in Chapter 4.

OTHER PROGRAMS THAT SUPPORT THE EDUCATION OF MIGRANT CHILDREN AND YOUTH

Besides the Migrant Education Program that is part of Title I of the Elementary and Secondary Schools Act, there are other educational support programs for which many migrant children and youth qualify. These include bilingual education programs, state and federally funded compensatory education programs, and special education services, as well as school breakfast and lunch programs.

For the many migrant children and youth whose first language is not English, bilingual education programs may be critical in providing real access to educational opportunities. Bilingual education is not new to the United States. The first state bilingual education law was enacted more than 160 years ago. In 1839, the state of Ohio adopted a bilingual education law that authorized education to be provided in English and

German for children of the state's large German immigrant population. Other states and territories soon followed suit; among them were Louisiana, which provided education in English and French, and the New Mexico Territory, which provided education in English and Spanish. According to an analysis by the National Association of Bilingual Educators (1998), "by the end of the nineteenth century, about a dozen states had passed similar laws. Elsewhere, many localities provided bilingual instruction without state sanction, in languages as diverse as Norwegian, Italian, Polish, Czech, and Cherokee" ("History of Bilingual Education" 1998, 1).

At the turn of the twentieth century, about 4 percent of public and parochial school students in the United States were participating in German-English programs. But even then, the language of instruction was connected to larger political issues. At the time of World War I, out of "fears about the loyalty of non-English speakers in general," several states enacted English-only legislation, even going so far as to "ban the study of foreign languages in the early grades" ("History of Bilingual Education" 1998, 1). Even though such bans on foreign-language instruction were declared unconstitutional in 1923, "by the mid-1920s, bilingual schooling was largely dismantled throughout the country" ("History of Bilingual Education" 1998, 1). English was the only language of instruction in the vast majority of classrooms in the United States.

In the 1960s, the civil rights movement and the large increases in immigration breathed new life into bilingual education, and the Bilingual Education Act, signed into law in 1968, provided federal funding for schools and school districts to investigate and provide instruction in students' first languages. This new bilingual education was bolstered by the 1974 U.S. Supreme Court decision in the *Lau v. Nichols* case (414 U.S. 563) that upheld the right of children to education in their first languages.

Lau v. Nichols, a class action suit, was brought against the San Francisco Unified School District on behalf of Chinese students who did not speak English. Lower courts had ruled that the school district was not responsible for the students' language deficiencies, but the Supreme Court disagreed. In a unanimous decision, the Court ruled that a school district's failure to provide instruction in students' primary languages denied those students their rightful access to a public education. The Supreme Court based its decision in part on regulations issued in 1970 by the U.S. Department of Health, Education, and Welfare for the implementation of the 1964 Civil Rights Act.

The Supreme Court quoted in its decision the regulatory guidance for the Civil Rights Act:

> Where inability to speak and understand the English language excludes
> national origin-minority group children from effective participation in
> the educational program offered by a school district, the district must
> take affirmative steps to rectify the language deficiency in order to
> open its instructional program to these students. Any ability grouping
> or tracking system employed by the school system to deal with the spe-
> cial language skill needs of national origin-minority group children
> must be designed to meet such language skill needs as soon as possible
> and must not operate as an educational dead end or permanent track.
> (*Lau v. Nichols* 1974, 414 U.S. 563)

In requiring "appropriate action" on the part of the school district, the
decision placed the responsibility for ensuring educational access for
language minority students with the school district. The decision did
not include specific remedies.

The Equal Opportunity Act of 1974 reflected the *Lau* decision.
Provisions of that legislation, part of the reauthorization of the Elementary and Secondary Schools Act, established an Office of Bilingual Education in the U.S. Office of Education, and initiated a number of activities related to bilingual education. The law established a National
Advisory Council on Bilingual Education and directed the National Institute of Education to conduct research on bilingual education. It provided
grants for research on bilingual education and for developing demonstration projects in bilingual education. The law authorized funds for
contracting with State Education Agencies (SEAs) to develop leadership
in bilingual education. Title VII of the Equal Opportunity Act Amendments also appropriated funds for bilingual vocational education.

Although the legislation did not set a legal standard for school districts' responsibilities to English language learners, case law did. In the
Casteñeda v. Pickard case (5th Cir. 1981), the courts established a legal
standard for the remedies missing in the *Lau* decision and in the Equal
Opportunity Act. The court's ruling in this case specified that "programs
for LEP [limited English proficient] students must be sound in theory,
provided with sufficient resources in practice, and monitored for effectiveness, with improvements made when necessary" (Crawford 1996, 2).
In 1975, the U.S. Department of Health, Education, and Welfare issued the
Lau Remedies, which required that elementary schools provide bilingual
instruction where enough LEP students made such a provision practical.

According to Crawford, "the Office for Civil Rights (OCR) began
an aggressive campaign to enforce the *Lau* Remedies, wielding the
threat (never exercised) of withholding federal funds to resistant school
districts" (Crawford 1996, 2). The OCR applied a three-step test in its re-

view of schools that served language minority students. OCR looked for schools to provide

>> Research-based programs that are viewed as theoretically sound by experts in the field
>> Adequate resources—such as staff, training, and materials— to implement the program
>> Standards and procedures to evaluate the program and a continuing obligation to modify a program that fails to meet results ("History of Bilingual Education" 1998, 1–2)

Crawford concluded that "the outcome [of the Office of Civil Rights' enforcement of the *Lau* Remedies], over the next five years, was the adoption of bilingual programs by nearly 500 districts that had previously neglected children's language needs. Without this intervention by OCR, bilingual education might well have remained, in much of the country, a marginal and experimental pedagogy" (Crawford 1996, 2).

Thus, by the end of the 1970s, even though there was no mandate in legislation at the federal level for it, bilingual education was fairly well established as a standard part of education in United States.

In the 1980s, the political climate for bilingual education changed. During the Reagan administration, funding for bilingual education under Title VII was reduced significantly. The OCR stopped enforcing the *Lau* Remedies, and instead reviewed school districts on a case-by-case basis. (The same anti-immigrant sentiment that brought about this reduction in bilingual education led to such initiatives as Proposition 187 in California that prohibited educational services to undocumented children and youth. Federal courts have since ruled such initiatives unconstitutional.)

The issue of bilingual education remains politically charged, both sides of the issue having strong, active, and vocal supporters. In 1998, for example, California voters passed Proposition 297; this proposition restricts the use of students' first languages (other than English) for instruction, and instead requires that schools provide structured English immersion for students whose first language is not English. Students may participate in structured English immersion for only one year. Parents may seek waivers that exempt their children from participating in structured English immersion classrooms; such waivers are required for students to participate in bilingual education or to receive language support for more than one year. Colorado and Massachusetts are among several other states that also limit the amount of time students may participate in language support programs.

Research on the length of time it takes for students to become proficient in English suggests that the amount of time varies from learner to learner. Garcia analyzed the literature related to second-language acquisition and found that the averages reported in the literature "mask very real variability in students' abilities, motivations, readiness, and opportunities to become sufficiently proficient in English to effectively succeed in mainstream all-English classrooms" (Garcia 2000, 3). Depending on the many variables in a student's home and school circumstances, according to Garcia, "an individual LEP student might acquire English to native-like proficiency levels in one to three years. Another LEP student might take from six to ten years to gain such proficiency" (Garcia 2000, 3). Because of such variability, enacting and enforcing arbitrary time limits has the potential to impede many students' English-language learning and consequently their success in school in general.

Today, bilingual education services are provided to many students whose first language is not English. Some schools provide ESL (English as a Second Language) programs; others provide dual-language programs; others involve students in immersion programs. Some schools provide separate newcomer classrooms or schools, where students who speak no English have opportunities to learn with other students who know little or no English. Some schools provide content instruction in a student's first language while they learn English; others explicitly teach English vocabulary within the context of content instruction; still others expect students to learn along with their English-proficient peers, with as little support as some minimal translation. There is no one accepted format for such services, but research points to four lessons learned from programs that are effective in helping LEP students to learn English. In effective second-language programs

- ➨ Educational services are tailored to the unique linguistic, cultural, and familial characteristics, and the academic learning needs of each LEP student.
- ➨ Some LEP students are provided instruction in their native languages on an as-needed basis as the foundation for learning age- and grade-appropriate English language arts and for learning core academic content in English.
- ➨ Teachers adjust instructional time to ensure the acquisition of the speaking and literacy skills that typical all-English classrooms require.
- ➨ When not fully proficient in English, LEP students are taught in alternative programs or groups before being transitioned into mainstream all-English classrooms. (Garcia 2000, 6, 7)

The program described in Chapter 6 shows how these lessons are being incorporated into schools and classrooms to support English-language learners.

EARLY CHILDHOOD AND FAMILY LITERACY PROGRAMS

Eligibility for the Migrant Education Program extends from age three through twenty-one. Some regular school programs include preschool education, and programs provided by other agencies may provide day care for children younger than three. In addition to such programs, two federally funded programs are specifically aimed at migrant preschoolers, Migrant Head Start (MHS) and Migrant Education Even Start (MEES).

In 1966, based on research that linked children's success in school with the socioeconomic status of their families, the U.S. Department of Health, Education, and Welfare initiated the Head Start program to provide comprehensive child development services, the goal being to increase the school readiness of young children from low-income families. Today, Head Start is administered through the U.S. Department of Health and Human Services. It is intended to give a head start, as its name implies, to the most disadvantaged children in the United States; its purpose is to provide these children the opportunity to start kindergarten and elementary school with the same knowledge and skills that their less disadvantaged peers enjoy. Head Start programs provide day care and educational, health, and nutrition services to the young children (from birth to age five) that they serve. Head Start programs also involve parents in the belief that parents are their children's first and most important teachers.

Head Start was officially extended to include programs aimed at addressing the specific needs of young children of migrant farmworkers in 1969. Providing Head Start programs to migrant children presents particular challenges. These challenges include designing programs that accommodate the migration of these families, communicating with families, and involving parents actively in the programs. According to Fuentes, Canto, and Stechuk (1996), MHS programs must be flexible to meet the needs of migrant families. The programs "may operate for as few as six weeks per calendar year, or for as long as nine to ten months. Individual MHS Centers may run from 8 [to] 12 hours per day for 5 [to] 7 days per week" (Fuentes, Canto, and Stechuk 1996, 16).

According to information from the Migrant Head Start Quality Improvement Center, which provides training, information, and technical assistance to Migrant Head Start programs, there are 400 Migrant Head Start centers located in thirty-four states. Together these centers serve approximately 37,000 children, over 35 percent of whom are infants and toddlers (MHS Quality Improvement Center 2000, 2).

Besides the educational, social, and health services provided by Head Start programs in general, Migrant Head Start programs are designed to meet the special needs of migrant families as they travel across the country. Migrant Head Start grantees fall into two categories: home-based grantees and upstream grantees. Home-based grantees are located in southern California, Arizona, New Mexico, and Florida, home states for many migrant families. These centers provide Head Start services to families while they are living at their home bases from October through May. Upstream grantees are located in states upstream from the home states: Washington, Idaho, Michigan, Illinois, Maine, Indiana, Wisconsin, Nebraska, and Minnesota. These centers open and provide Head Start services to migrant families as they move in search of seasonal farmwork in the spring, summer, and fall months (MHS Quality Improvement Center 2000).

A second program that provides early childhood education to migrant children is the Migrant Education Even Start Program, authorized with the 1988 reauthorization of the ESEA; Migrant Education Even Start funded programs for the first time in 1989. Even Start broadens the scope of the program beyond early childhood education to include family literacy; its policies are based on research that shows the level of parents' education is a strong predictor of children's success in school. Even Start programs focus on family literacy through three components: early childhood education, adult literacy or adult basic education, and parenting education. The Migrant Education Even Start Program, administered through the U.S. Department of Education Office of Migrant Education, provides grants for up to forty-eight months to states, local education agencies, and other organizations that work with migrant families to begin these family literacy programs. Unlike Head Start, which is fully funded at the federal level, Even Start programs require matching funds; the federal grant for a Migrant Education Even Start program is not more than 90 percent the first year, 80 percent the second, 70 percent the third, and 60 percent the fourth year, the intention being that these programs will become state or locally funded as they become established.

Migrant Education Even Start programs focus on integrated family literacy. Families in the programs participate in early childhood education, adult education, and parenting education. In Migrant Education Even Start programs, the adult education component is often adult English as a Second Language (ESL) or adult basic education with the goal of preparation for the GED (general equvalency diploma). Like other Even Start programs, Migrant Education Even Start serves children from birth to the age of seven; it serves their families through home visits, site-based instruction, and site-based family meetings. Parents served by Migrant Even Start programs must be eligible for participation under the Adult Education Act. In fiscal year 1999, sixteen Migrant Education Even Start programs were operating through grants totaling $3,449,760 (Catalog of Federal Domestic Assistance 2000, 84.214, 3).

The design of each Migrant Education Even Start program varies and is based on the needs of the families served by the program, the collaborating partners, and the resources of the community. The twelve programs funded in 2000 are based in Arizona, California, Hawaii, Illinois, Kansas, Maine, Nebraska, North Carolina, Texas, and Vermont.

Several of the Migrant Education Even Start programs are multi-site programs that provide services to families as they migrate. One such program is SERVE/UNC-Project ASPIRE. According to a program description provided by the Office of Migrant Education, Project ASPIRE provides services throughout the western migrant stream of Florida. The Binational Migrant Education Even Start project focuses on families who travel between Pennsylvania and Mexico. This project is based on a collaborative relationship established between Pennsylvania and the Mexican Department of Education. This collaboration facilitates year-round family literacy services that depend on "similar textbooks, teacher exchanges, native-language literacy and adult education models, and international credit transfers. Technology, such as e-mail, Internet, and televised instruction for adult education, will connect families whether they are in Mexico or Pennsylvania" (Office of Migrant Education 2000, 1–2). Other Migrant Education Even Start programs use such innovative strategies as including employers as partners in workplace literacy components, being located in housing projects where participants reside, and involving customized plans (such as technology) to continue services to families as they migrate from work site to work site.

SUPPORT FOR SECONDARY AND POSTSECONDARY EDUCATION

Migrant children and youth are especially at risk of dropping out of high school or not completing enough course credits to graduate because of their migrant lifestyle. With the high rates of migrant youth either dropping out or not graduating from high school, it is not surprising that migrant youth are underrepresented in postsecondary education. As with other underserved youth, several factors contribute to this situation. For migrant youth, those factors are compounded by their migrant lifestyle. According to Morse and Hammer, "To succeed in college, migrant students must (1) complete high school with adequate preparation for college, (2) apply and be accepted to college, (3) find scholarships or other funding to attend, and (4) progress through college to graduation" (Morse and Hammer 1998, 1).

The Migrant Education Program includes programs that are designed not only to help migrant students complete high school and be prepared for entrance into postsecondary education programs but also to help them be successful once they have been admitted into postsecondary programs. The High School Equivalency Program (HEP), and the College Assistance Migrant Program (CAMP), are two parts of the Migrant Education Program that are aimed specifically at helping migrant students succeed in postsecondary education. Both HEP and CAMP were originally funded and administered through the U.S. Department of Labor; funding for the two programs began in 1967. HEP and CAMP are currently authorized through Public Law 102–325 (1992), which amended and reauthorized the Higher Education Act (HEA) of 1965.

HEP programs are funded by grants to colleges and universities, or to nonprofit organizations that collaborate with colleges and universities, to provide academic and support services to migrant youth and their families and to aid migrant students in completing high school or GED programs. Support services in HEP programs may include counseling, health services, stipends for participants, education placement, and job placement. These programs must be designed not only to assist migrant students in completing their GEDs but also to provide assistance that prepares migrant student for entrance into postsecondary education, job training programs, or the workforce. To be eligible for HEP services, a migrant youth must be at least sixteen years old and lacking a high school diploma or its equivalent. HEP programs are currently offered in California, Colorado, Florida, Idaho, Maryland, Mississippi, New Mexico, Oregon, Puerto Rico, Tennessee, Texas, Washington, and Wisconsin.

CAMP is designed to provide support to undergraduate migrant students. Through grants to colleges and universities, or to nonprofit organizations that collaborate with colleges and universities, CAMP projects offer services that include tutoring, counseling, health services, assistance with admission, and some financial assistance to migrant students. These services are aimed at helping migrant students complete their first year of postsecondary education. CAMP projects also help migrant students to obtain financial aid to support the rest of their undergraduate education. CAMP projects are currently in operation in California, Colorado, Georgia, Idaho, Pennsylvania, Puerto Rico, and Texas.

Both HEP and CAMP programs have been very successful in supporting migrant youth in completing high school and going on to postsecondary education. The president of the HEP/CAMP Association reported that the number of HEP and CAMP sites will grow to nearly eighty in 2001.

Another program that has been in place since 1978 to assist migrant youth in accruing the credits necessary to graduate from high school is the Portable Assisted Study Sequence, or PASS program. The PASS program originated in California as part of a Secondary School Migrant Dropout Prevention Program (New York State PASS Program 1998, 4). The PASS program was designed to provide students with opportunities to continue working toward completing the course credits they need to graduate as they travel from school to school and from state to state. PASS consists of "self-contained, semi-independent study courses which enable students to earn secondary-level credits for high school graduation" (National PASS Center 2000, 1). The PASS courses are competency-based; students complete activity books developed for each course, as well as the tests that accompany them, at their own pace (National PASS Center 2000, 1). Some middle school-level courses are also offered as part of the program. These courses are labeled Mini-PASS. Summer school programs for migrant youth of high school age are often designed to provide tutoring and instruction that help students complete their coursework through PASS as they travel from their home school districts.

ADULT EDUCATION

Designing programs that address the needs of migrant adults involves many of the same challenges as those presented in designing programs for migrant children and youth: mobility, cultural dissonance, language barriers, and health care issues. Like their children, adult migrants experience educational discontinuity when they move from one educational program to another. Because there is little intra- or interstate coordination of adult education programs, the discontinuity may be even greater. To further interfere with continuing their educations, migrant adults work long hours and are often exhausted; they face difficulties with child care and transportation; and those who are undocumented face the additional fear of being detected by immigration authorities and possibly deported. There are no organized interstate efforts to maintain and transfer the educational records of adult migrants. Consequently, when migrants do participate in adult education programs, a disproportionate amount of time may be taken up with testing and other diagnostic procedures, leaving less time for teaching and learning.

Since 1986, the funding of literacy education for many farmworkers (who were given legal status through the amnesty provided by the Special Agricultural Workers Legalization Program) has been provided through State Legalization Impact Assistance Grants (SLIAG). In addition, the 1988 Adult Education Act, Section 372 of Public Law 100–297, authorized funding for literacy and English-language education for adults and out-of-school youth. Since that time, various adult education programs have been developed to serve migrant workers.

The successful programs have used a variety of delivery models to meet the specific needs of the adult migrants they serve, but they share a set of characteristics identified by Bartlett and Vargas in their 1991 analysis of adult migrant education programs. These characteristics include

- ➡ Participatory or learner-centered programs that involve learners in goal setting and selecting course content
- ➡ Activities that build learners' confidence in their own learning
- ➡ Program personnel who are bilingual and culturally sensitive
- ➡ Scheduling that is flexible
- ➡ Support and social services (such as transportation, child care, food assistance, health care, and immigration and legal assistance) that address the barriers faced by the students (Bartlett and Vargas 1991, 2–3)

The 1998 Workforce Investment Act (Public Law 105–220) and the 1998 Adult and Family Literacy Act bring together services that address needs of adult migrants. This legislation provides for the integration of federal employment, adult education, and vocational rehabilitation programs to create an integrated, one-stop system of workforce investment and education activities for adults and youth. Migrant Education Even Start programs also provide adult education as part of family literacy and coordinated social and support services as described earlier. Chapter 4 includes the description of an adult migrant education program that represents the characteristics outlined by Bartlett and Vargas.

INTERSTATE COORDINATION AND COLLABORATION

From its inception, the Migrant Education Program took as one of its primary objectives the alleviation of the educational discontinuity that migrant children and youth face as they move from school to school. In the REA/NCALL demonstration project in the 1950s, for example, this discontinuity was addressed by employing teachers who moved with migrant students as they traveled from state to state, school to school. With the exception of such efforts as the Migrant Student Record Transfer System (MSRTS) and the New Generation System (NGS), little provision was made for interstate coordination and collaboration in the federal legislation that supported the Migrant Education Program until the authorization.

Current migrant education program legislation, the Improving America's Schools Act, provides for grants to support intrastate consortia. The South Dakota Migrant Education Program explains that "any state, regardless of the amount of such state's allocation, may submit a consortium arrangement for approval. A consortium arrangement with another state or appropriate entity should result in (a) a reduction of administrative costs or program function costs for state programs and (b) make more funds available for direct services to add substantially to the welfare or educational attainment of children to be served under Title I, Part C" (South Dakota Department of Education 2001).

This provision in the legislation allows for the development of value-added programs, particularly important for states whose resources for migrant education programs are limited because of small allocations. The Improving America's Schools Act provisions for the Migrant Education Program set aside up to $6 million for grants or contracts to improve the interstate or intrastate coordination of services to migrant children.

An additional $1.5 million is also reserved for the establishment of consortia to reduce state administrative costs for the migrant education program. According to the U.S. Office of Migrant Education, current collaborative projects address identification and recruitment, the administration of out-of-state testing for students whose home base is in another state, distance learning and technology, and the multistate development of assessment instruments to improve the academic placement of migrant students in core academic subjects. Examples of such interstate coordination and collaboration are described in Chapter 4.

BINATIONAL MIGRANT EDUCATION PROGRAMS

As discussed in Chapter 1, migrant education is not only a national concern. Because a substantial number of farmworkers and their families migrate between the United States and Mexico each year, migrant education is also an international concern. The differences between the educational systems of the Untied States and Mexico, as noted in Chapter 1, may contribute to educational discontinuity for these students, as well as to difficulties in accruing credits for graduation. These issues have been recognized by educators in Mexico and in the United States; as early as the 1970s, binational efforts were underway to support students who migrate between schools in the United States and Mexico. In the 1970s, a formal dialogue between Mexican and Mexican American educators began, but, according to Miller, "differences among the organizations [the Mexican American educators represented] in the United States prevented any institutional [or formal] relationship from developing" (Miller 1996, 104).

Meetings between educators in the two countries continued, however, and in 1980, formal collaboration between the United States and Mexico began with a meeting in Mexico City of the Association of Mexican American Educators. This meeting provided the impetus for the development of several binational programs. According to Miller, "Mexican teachers went to Los Angeles and Louisiana, training programs were held for bilingual teachers from the Los Angeles area, bilingual programs in San Jose (California) used Mexican textbooks, and Mexican officials became visiting scholars in the United States" (Miller 1996, 105).

In 1982, an official Binational Program between California and Michoacàn began. This program supported research that identified educational issues faced by children and youth who migrated across the border from Mexico to California and back. In particular, the research focused on the accrual of academic credit and the transfer of that credit between schools in one country and schools in the other. As a result of this work, a Binational Transfer Document was developed. This document helps to simplify the transfer of students, as well as credit they have earned, between Mexico and several states in the United States. To register at participating schools, according to Miller, a student must have a birth certificate and a transfer document validated with the binational seal. Students with proper documentation are accepted at any time of the year in the Mexican schools and are placed at the same grade level they were in at the school they had attended in the United States (Miller 1996, 108).

This binational agreement has reduced the amount of time spent testing students when they return to and enroll in schools in Mexico; it has also helped to ensure that students are placed at the proper grade levels. Before the agreement, students often faced lengthy diagnostic testing processes and then placement at lower grade levels than those they had been assigned to in the schools they had left in the United States.

The Mexican government established a program in 1990 that would help Mexican Americans understand their Mexican heritage. The Program for Mexican Communities Abroad was established by Mexican president Carlos Salinas to link communities that have significant populations of Mexican Americans with communities in Mexico. Administered through the Mexican State Department, the Mexican Ministry of Education, and Mexican consulates in the United States, the program has established a series of Mexican cultural institutes. The program continues to provide educational curriculum and materials to schools in the U.S. communities, and supports the exchange of teachers between the communities. Currently, the program operates in twenty-one cities in eleven states and the District of Columbia in the United States. A description of the educational activities the Mexican Cultural and Educational Institute of Chicago sponsors and is involved in is found in Chapter 4. A list of the Mexican Cultural and Educational Institutes in the United States is found in Chapter 7.

In 1990, U.S. secretary of education Lauro Cavazos and Mexican secretary of education Manuel Bartlett-Diaz signed a Memorandum of Agreement to establish educational ties between the two countries. The original agreement extended through 1991, but several extensions of the agreement have been signed since then. Several exchange activities have been conducted under this agreement, including a border conference that was held in 1991. The memorandum "encourage[s] and facilitate[s] relationships that emphasize exchanges and dialogue centered on educational management, methods, evaluation and research. Emphasis in the agreement is on bilateral initiatives and programs, and the study and teaching of each other's language, culture, and history through the development of exchanges and cooperative activities" (Habermann 1997, 1).

Education and migration issues have been and are being discussed at the cabinet level between the U.S. and Mexican governments. As a result of groundwork laid by U.S. president Jimmy Carter and Mexican president Lopez Portillo begun in 1977, a Binational Commission was established in 1981 by President Ronald Reagan and President Lopez Portillo. This Binational Commission allows for regular exchanges at the cabinet level of the two countries, and includes fifteen working groups, among them a group focused on education and cultural affairs, and another on migration and consular affairs.

Some states, among them California, New Mexico, Michigan, Florida, and Texas, have established programs that support cooperation and collaboration with Mexico. The New Mexico State Board of Education, for example, adopted a resolution in 1992 that called for cooperation with Mexico in developing policies related to education, and in 1993, "State Board of Education members met with education officials from Mexico and jointly propose[d] official ties between education agencies of Nuevo Leon and New Mexico. These encompassed teacher exchanges and various collaborative efforts in the areas of research into elementary and secondary education, reciprocity for teacher certification, joint professional development activities, and technology" (Habermann 1997, 8).

One component that developed out of this cooperation is a teacher exchange that began in 1995. Objectives for the teacher exchange include to

- ➡ Develop understanding about the education systems of the United States/Mexico
- ➡ Promote closer international education ties among teachers, schools, districts, and state education agencies
- ➡ Promote understanding and good will among professionals involved in the education of children on both sides of the border
- ➡ Share methodology, instructional materials, and models of dual-language instruction
- ➡ Provide workshops and co-teach in a classroom setting (Habermann 1997, 15)

Teachers from New Mexico travel to Nuevo Leon, Mexico, to teach for two weeks, and then host their Mexican colleagues as they teach for two weeks in a New Mexico school. These teachers not only visit each others' classrooms; they also stay in their exchange partners' homes during their visits.

Mary Jean Habermann surveyed teachers who participated in the 1996 teacher exchange and found that they had gained a much greater understanding of students who go to school on both sides of the border. One teacher wrote,

> There were more similarities than differences. Therefore, we need to concentrate and communicate on what is shared so that we can create

> a common basis of expectancies to facilitate cross border work. . . . This
> will ensure that students' education does not suffer in crossing. . . .
> (Habermann 1997, 13)

Another teacher described learning strategies from her exchange partner that she could use immediately, not only to help her students learn
but also to make a home-school connection with families who crossed
the border.

> My exchange partner-teacher happened to be teaching the same topic
> in Math as I was. She showed my students the Mexican method for di-
> vision and my students really related to their division problems without
> hesitation. In addition, my other bilingual children made me aware
> [that] that is how their parents were showing them at home as they
> tried to help . . . with their homework. Now, I will definitely teach divi-
> sion using both strategies. (Habermann 1997, 14)

Programs such as this one in New Mexico show how important such exchanges can be to the success of children who must negotiate their participation in both educational systems. Binational programs between
Mexico and the states of New Mexico, Florida, Texas, Pennsylvania,
Michigan, among other states, have the potential not only to help teachers gain a better understanding of what students experience as they travel
across the border but also to help teachers redesign their classrooms to
help children negotiate their transfers from one system to the other.

TRANSFER OF RECORDS

The issue of records transfer is not only an international issue; it is also
critical for students who migrate within the United States. Maintaining
accurate student academic and health records for migrant children and
youth, as well as transferring them in time to facilitate students' educational placement as they travel, is an issue that has been addressed by
the Migrant Education Program since its beginning. The 1966 Migrant
Education Program Amendments included a provision for the transfer
of student records, and in 1969, MSRTS was initiated for this purpose.
MSRTS, a national database, was operated under contracts with the
Arkansas Department of Education. Local schools provided student academic and health records to MSRTS through a series of data centers located in areas where there were high concentrations of migrant students. Once student data were entered into the system, schools could

access that information by contacting the MSRTS, which would send reports through the mail. This system was designed also to provide information that could be aggregated to provide information at the program and state levels, both for program planning and for evaluation (Cahape 1993, 1).

In 1988, Congress established a National Commission on Migrant Education (NCME). Part of the charge to the commission was to evaluate the effectiveness of MSRTS. While recognizing that MSRTS was the "first and only national database serving migrant students" (Cahape 1993, 1), NCME concluded that the system had become unwieldy as its focus had shifted from transfer of individual student records to program planning and evaluation; concerns were also expressed about the cost effectiveness of MSRTS. The recommendations for improvement included easier access for local educators and an increased role for parents in MSRTS, as well as the call for an assessment of the program's cost effectiveness (Cahape 1993, 3).

In the 1994 Improving American's Schools Act, the Migrant Education Program statute included a mandate to replace MSRTS, and at the same time required "more attention to records transfer than did the previous statute" (Wright 1995, 3). To meet that need, a consortium of twenty-nine states issued an RFP (request for proposals and bids) for the development of a new system. In spring 1995, a team at Texas A & M University in Kingsville, Texas, began the development of what would become the NGS, an Internet-based system intended to be "user-friendly" and fast (NGS 1996).

At the same time, the U.S. Department of Education National Center for Education Statistics and the Office of Migrant Education initiated the Migrant/Mobile School Locator Demonstration project (1998). This demonstration project, which initially worked in collaboration with NGS, sought to develop a solution to the problem of communication across the different electronic databases used by states to maintain and communicate migrant student academic and health records. According to the final report of the project, "there are no major technical barriers to overcome to implement a nationwide locator solution. . . . It can support the electronic transfer of the actual student record" (Office of Migrant Education 1998, 4).

Currently, no one vehicle exists to facilitate the transfer of migrant student records, and schools use several different means of doing so. In their survey of schools that serve migrant students in schoolwide projects, Siler, Stolzberg, von Glatz, and Strang found that most schools "obtained and sent the cumulative records of newly enrolled migrant students by mail, with fewer reporting that they used fax, phone, or electronic methods" (Siler et al. 1999a, 51). Recommendations for the next reauthorization of the Migrant Education Program include increasing support for interstate records transfer (Department of Education 1999, 1). In other words, finding an efficient and effective method of transferring student records still has not been resolved for the Migrant Education Program. According to the Migrant/Mobile School Locator Demonstration project, there are no barriers to the electronic transfer of records, even between different database systems. Finding a way to link all the systems that gather and organize data may be the challenge.

TECHNICAL ASSISTANCE FOR MIGRANT EDUCATION PROGRAMS

Technical assistance has been provided to migrant education programs from a variety of sources. Until 1996, three Program Coordination Centers provided technical assistance to migrant education programs. There was one center for each of the three streams of migration. The Eastern Stream Coordination Center was at the State University of New York at Oneonta; the Central Stream Coordination Center was at Texas A & I University in Brownsville; and the Western Stream Coordination Center was in Beaverton, Oregon. The purpose of these centers was to promote coordination between and among states and schools that served migrant students and continuity of educational programs for migrant students (Kindler 1995, 9). There was also a network of Technical Assistance Centers (TACs) and Rural Technical Assistance Centers (RTACs) that were funded by the ESEA and provided assistance in program development, program improvement, and program evaluation to state and local school districts for compensatory education programs, including the Migrant Education Program, as well as a network of Title VII Multifunctional Resource Centers that provided technical assistance for bilingual education. All these centers provided professional development in effective curriculum, instruction, and assessment for Migrant Education Program teachers.

The Improving America's Schools Act (1994) replaced the coordination centers, TACs, RTACs, and multifunctional resource centers with fifteen comprehensive regional assistance centers that currently provide technical assistance to migrant education programs. Other sources of technical assistance are the ten Regional Education Laboratories; the National Diffusion Network, which identifies and disseminates information about exemplary education programs; the Regional Technical

Support and Professional Development Consortia for Technology, which provide assistance in the use and integration of technology into educational programs; the Eisenhower Regional Mathematics and Science Education Consortia; and the National Clearinghouse for Bilingual Education (Migrant Education Program 1995a, 2, 3).

MIGRANT HEALTH SERVICES

Chapter 1 described the complex health problems faced by migrant farm workers and their families. These health problems are compounded by the difficulties migrant families face in accessing health care. In 1962, the Migrant Health Act was passed "partly out of concern for the plight of farmworkers, partly to protect farm community residents from communicable diseases, and partly to assist an overburdened rural health care system" (National Health Service Corps 2000).

Currently, the U.S. Department of Health and Human Services administers the Migrant Health Program by providing grants to more than 120 community and state organizations for primary health care services to migrant workers and their families. The Migrant Health Clinics funded under this program offer services in ways that address the unique health care needs of migrant families; service, for example, may be offered at migrant camps, and health care workers may be bilingual. Chapter 4 includes the description of one migrant health clinic's efforts to address migrant families' health care needs.

EQUITY

The Migrant Education Program has been based on creating educational opportunities for migrant students. In 1992, the Migrant Education Goals Task Force of the National Association of State Directors of Migrant Education (NASDME) wrote a response to the National Education Goals and America 2000. The response, much of which was drawn from a series of forums held in Buffalo, New York, during the 1991 National Conference on Migrant and Seasonal Farmworkers, is centered around a mission of working toward equity for migrant children. "Our mission as educators of migrant children is to ensure that all efforts to achieve the National Education Goals will equitably include all migrant children" (NASDME 1992, 5)

The task force outlined twelve expectations for the education of migrant children and youth that, if enacted, would ensure parity with students who are traditionally successful in school. The expectations for equity set by the Migrant Education Goals Task Force are:

Expectation One: Migrant children should enter first grade fully prepared to learn and schools should be fully prepared to help them learn.

Expectation Two: The cultural and language diversity represented by migrant students should be used positively and creatively within schools and communities.

Expectation Three: Between 1992 and 2002, the number of migrant students graduating from high school should increase annually by 10 percent.

Expectation Four: Migrant students should complete the elementary grades with mastery of critical skills in learning to read, write, compute, and think.

Expectation Five: Migrant students should complete the middle school grades, be able to reason critically, and understand the relevance to their lives of the subject matter they are learning.

Expectation Six: Migrant students entering high school should be able to complete their educations and graduate successfully.

Expectation Seven: Migrant students should be provided stimulating learning experiences in science, mathematics, and technology education as they proceed through their school years.

Expectation Eight: The academic achievement of migrant students should be at a level that will enable them upon graduation from high school to be prepared for postsecondary education, employment, or both.

Expectation Nine: Migrant students who do not choose college should be provided school-to-work transition experiences so they leave high school prepared with the skills necessary to participate productively in the world of work and with the foundation required to upgrade their skills and advance their employment and career opportunities.

Expectation Ten: Adults and out-of-school migrant youth should be provided quality experiences and opportunities to improve their literacy, basic education, and problem-solving skills.

Expectation Eleven: Migrant children should attend schools that are free of drugs and alcohol and where students are well nourished and healthy, feel safe, and learn in a supportive and caring environment.

Expectation Twelve: Every state department of education should have a successful comprehensive strategy for migrant children and youth that provides a process to bring about quality, equity, and congruence in their education. (NASDME 1992, 5)

The report continues with an analysis of the U.S. educational system as it addresses migrant children and youth in relationship to the six national goals. For each of the goals, the report offers recommendations in the form of opportunities for innovation, opportunities for reflection, and opportunities for action which, if enacted, would have the potential to bring about equity of outcomes for migrant education. Unfortunately, for many migrant students, such equity is still only a dream.

From its beginnings in a few local programs designed to meet the educational needs of migrant children who lived in the community for only part of the year, to its status as a federally funded educational program and the focus of binational attention, the Migrant Education Program has worked to address the unique educational needs of migrant families, their children, and their youth. But even after thirty-five years of the Migrant Education Program, there is still work to be done. For many migrant children and youth, the barriers to education remain the same. Children, in growing numbers, face educational discontinuity. Many of them drop out of school and have few options for work outside the migrant labor force; and so the cycle of poverty and undereducation continues.

In April 2001, migrant educators, parents, and students met to celebrate the thirty-fifth anniversary of the Migrant Education Program. At this thirty-third annual conference, sponsored by NASDME, migrant educators from all fifty states, the District of Columbia, and Puerto Rico shared their concerns for the reauthorization process going on concurrently in the U.S. Congress. The sentiment in Congress to eliminate categorical programs when it reauthorizes the Elementary and Secondary Education Act could eliminate funding currently earmarked specifically for the Migrant Education Program. Although the program has traditionally been underfunded, its survival as a categorical program for thirty-five years has required that SEAs, school districts, and schools address the educational needs of migrant children and their families. If the Migrant Education Program loses its categorical status, then federal funds will not be allocated specifically for a Migrant Education Program. If that happens, migrant educators worry that these children's unique educational needs will no longer be addressed.

This chapter has provided a historical look at the Migrant Education Program, how it has been shaped by the legislation that authorized and reauthorized it, and how its components have developed. It has also discussed some of the support and ancillary services that have developed around the Migrant Education Program. Chapter 4 will describe how some of the various components are currently being implemented in states, school districts, and schools across the country.

REFERENCES

Bartlett, K. J., and F. O. Vargas. "Literacy Education for Adult Migrant Farmworkers." *ERIC Digest*. Washington, DC: National Clearinghouse on Literacy Education, 1991. Available: http://www.cal.org/NCLE/Digests/LIT_EDUCATION.html

Cahape, P. "The Migrant Student Record Transfer System (MSRTS): An Update." *ERIC Digest*. Charleston, WV: ERIC Clearinghouse on Rural Education and Small Schools, 1993. (ERIC Document Reproduction Service No. 357909)

Catalog of Federal Domestic Assistance. *84.214: Even Start: Migrant Education,* 2000. Available: http://aspe.os.dhhs.gov/cfda/Pi4214.htm

Crawford, J. "Summing Up the Lau Decision: Justice Is Never Simple." *Revisiting the Lau Decision—20 Years After: Proceedings of a National Commemorative Symposium Held on November 3–4, 1994, in San Francisco, California.* Oakland, CA: ARC Associates, 1996. Available: http://ourworld.compuserve.com/homepages/JWCRAWFORD/summing.htm

DiCerbo, P. A. "Why Migrant Education Matters." *Issue & Brief No. 8.* Washington, DC: National Clearinghouse for Bilingual Education Center for the Study of Language & Education, 2001. Available: http://www/ncbe.gwu.edu

Fuentes, F., V. D. Cantu, R. Stechuk. "Migrant Head Start: What Does It Mean to Involve Parents in Program Services?" *Children Today* 24, no. 1 (1996): 16–18.

Garcia, G. N. "Lessons from Research: What Is the Length of Time It Takes Limited English Proficient Students to Acquire English and Success in an All-English Classroom?" *Issue & Brief No. 5.* Washington, DC: National Clearinghouse for Bilingual Education Center for the Study of Language & Education, 2000. Available: http://www.ncbe.gwu.edu

Habermann, M. J. "Binational Teacher Development: Teacher Ambassador Exchange Program, New Mexico, USA, and Nuevo Leon, Mexico." Paper presented at the Annual Meeting of the National Association for Bilingual Education, February 1997. (ERIC Document Reproduction Service No. 404884)

"History of Bilingual Education." *Rethinking Schools* 12, no. 3 (spring 1998): 1, 2. Available: http://www.rethinkingschools.org/Archives/12_03/langhst.htm

Kindler, A. L. "Education of Migrant Children in the United States." *Directions in Language & Education* 1, no. 8 (1995): 1–11.

Lau v. Nichols, 414 U.S. 563, 1974.

McGeehan, J. H. "A Migrant Summer School." In *Another "Disadvantaged" Dimension: Educating the Migrant Child,* edited by A. F. Pinney, 119–120. Cheyney, PA: Cheyney State College, 1969.

Migrant Education Program. *Preliminary Guidance for Migrant Education Program, Title I, Part C Public Law 103–382: Appendix A—Resources for Technical Assistance.* Washington, DC: Migrant Education Program, 1995a. Available: http://www.ed.gov/offices/OESE/MEP/PrelimGuide/appendix.html

———. *Preliminary Guidance for Migrant Education Program, Title I, Part C Public Law 103–382: A Focus on Teaching and Learning.* Washington, DC: Migrant Education Program, 1995b. Available: http://www.ed.gov/offices/OESE/MEP/PrelimGuide/pt3.html

———. *Preliminary Guidance for Migrant Education Program, Title I, Part C Public Law 103–382: Interstate, Intrastate, and Interagency Coordination.* Washington, DC: Migrant Education Program, 1995c. Available: http://www.ed.gov/offices/OESE/MEP/ PrelimGuide/pt1c.html

———. *Preliminary Guidance for Migrant Education Program, Title I, Part C Public Law 103–382: Serving Migrant Children in Schoolwide Programs.* Washington, DC: Migrant Education Program, 1995d. Available: http://www.ed.gov/offices/OESE/MEP/Prelim Guide/pt3a.html

Migrant Head Start (MHS) Quality Improvement Center. *Region XII Head Start/Migrant Head Start,* 2000. Available: http://216.219.150.126

Miller, R. "Mexico's Role in U.S. Education—A Well-Kept Secret." *Phi Delta Kappan* 76, no. 6 (1995): 470–474.

Morse, S., and P. C. Hammer. *Migrant Students Attending College: Facilitating Their Success.* Charleston, WV: Clearinghouse on Rural Education and Small Schools, 1998. (ERIC Document Reproduction Service No. ED 423097)

National Association of State Directors of Migrant Education (NASDME). *Rethinking Migrant Education.* Baltimore: Migrant Education Goals Task Force, 1992.

National Committee on the Education of Migrant Children. *Wednesday's Children.* New York: National Committee on the Education of Migrant Children, 1971.

National Health Service Corps. "Migrant Health," 2000. Available: http//www.bphc.hrsa.gov/nhsc/Pages/about_nhsc/3D1b_migrant.htm

National PASS Center. *What Is PASS?* Mt. Morris, NY: National PASS Center, 2000. Available: http://www.migrant.net/pass/index.htm

New Generation System Office (NGS). *New Generation System: An Interstate Information Network Serving America's Children.* Kingsville, TX: New Generation System Office, 1966. (ERIC Document Reproduction Service No. 396877)

New York State PASS Program. 1998. Available: www.oneonta.edu/~hickeysa/ pass.html #add

Office of Education (DHEW). *Report of Title I, ESEA, Migrant Coordinators Meeting.* Washington, DC: Office of Education (DHEW), Bureau of Elementary and Secondary Education, 1969. (ERIC Document Reproduction Service No. 039056)

Office of Migrant Education. *Report on the Findings from the Migrant/Mobile School Locator Demonstration Project.* Washington, DC: Office of Migrant Education, 1998. Available: html://www.ed.gov/offices/OESE/ MEP/PrelimGuide/locator.html

———. Even Start Project Summaries. Washington, DC: Office of Migrant Education, 2000. Available: http://www.ed.gov/offices/ OESE/MEP/meesfy00. html

Parsad, B., S. Heaviside, C. Williams, and E. Farris. *Title I Migrant Education Program Summer Term Projects, 1998.* Washington, DC: U.S. Department of Education Office of Educational Research and Improvement, National Center for Education Statistics, 2000.

SHARE Consortium. *Migrant Leadership Academy: Academy 2000 Report.* Monett, MO: SHARE Consortium, 2000.

Siler, A., S. Stolzberg, A. van Glatz, and W. Strang. *Meeting the Needs of Migrant Students in Schoolwide Programs: Technical Report of the Congressionally Mandated Study of Migrant Student Participation in Schoolwide Programs.* Rockville, MD: Westat, 1999a.

———. Executive Summary. *Meeting the Needs of Migrant Students in Schoolwide Programs: Technical Report of the Congressionally Mandated Study of Migrant Student Participation in Schoolwide Programs.* Rockville, MD: Westat, 1999b.

South Dakota Department of Education. Consortium Agreements. *Migrant Education Program, 2001.* Available: http://www.state.sd.us/deca/TA/programs/cair.htm

Stockburger, C. *The Impact of Interstate Programs on Continuity in Migrant Education.* Las Cruces, NM: New Mexico State University, Clearinghouse on Rural Education and Small Schools (CRESS), 1980. (ERIC Document Reproduction Service No. 184783)

U.S. Department of Education. "Identification and Recruitment." Preliminary Guidance for Migrant Education Program, Title I, Part C Public Law 103–382, 1996a. Available: www.ed.gov/offices/OESE/MEP/PrelimGuide/ pt2a.html

———. "A Focus on Teaching and Learning." Preliminary Guidance for Migrant Education Program, Title I, Part C Public Law 103–382, 1996b. Available: http://www.ed.gov/offices/OESE/MEP/PrelimGuide/pt.3.html

———. *Title I, Part C—Education of Migratory Children.* Washington, D.C.: U.S. Department of Education, 1999. Available: http://search.ed.gov/results

Wright, A. "Reauthorized Migrant Education Program: Old Themes and New." *ERIC Digest.* Charleston, WV: ERIC Clearinghouse on Rural Education and Small Schools, 1995. (ERIC Document Reproduction Service No. 380267)

Chapter Four

❧ Migrant Education Programs Today

A Street Kid's Guide

It's hard to get from here to there
If you never get out of bed.
You lie a lot to fool your friends
But you fooled yourself instead.
It's hard to get from here to there
If you set your goals too high;
Then nothing ever works out right;
Too soon, you no longer try.
But the hardest way to get from here to there
Is when all you ever do
Is count up the years, and miles to go.
Then you're through before you're through.
So how do you get from here to there?
Well, first you must believe you can
Let no one tell you differently—
It's your life and it's in your hands.
Then turn your dreams into your goals
And see what it is you need now
To satisfy the requirements:
The why, the where and how.
At first you're overwhelmed, of course;
There is so much you don't know.
But keep your faith, be strong, be sure,
For you do have a way to go.
Take careful steps and do them right,
Take pride in each thing done.
Don't look far ahead of yourself,
Just that next step yet to come.
Before you know it you'll be there,

Your dream will then be real.
And you'll be standing where I am now,
Telling others how good it feels.
You'll tell them not to quit themselves,
To have faith, though it's hard to bear.
So they will know it can be done-
They, too, can get from here to there.
—Pilar, La Joya, Texas, and Champaign, Illinois (1999, 11)

Pilar, a high school student, migrates each year between Illinois and a home base in Texas. In spite of the obstacles that she has had to face because of her family's migrant lifestyle, Pilar's poem represents the incredible resilience, determination, and persistence that have enabled her to continue to work at her education and succeed where so many other youth have failed. For Pilar, the Migrant Education Program has been a safety net, providing opportunities to fill in the gaps that migrating might have left in her educational program.

Chapter 3 described the development of the federally funded Migrant Education Program from its beginnings prior to the 1966 Migrant Education Program Amendment to the Elementary and Secondary Schools Act of 1965 and its reauthorizations, as well as a number of other programs and support services intended to address the barriers that migrant workers and their children face as they deal with education and schooling. This chapter explains how the provisions of the Migrant Education Program and other educational and support services are currently being implemented, and how states, schools, and school districts in the United States are working to address the needs of migrant children, youth, and their families. It will also describe how the United States, several state departments of education, and the government of Mexico are collaborating to address the special needs of the migrant children and youth who travel between schools in the United States and Mexico.

The Migrant Education Program is currently operating under the authority of Title I, Part C of the Improving America's Schools Act (IASA), enacted in 1994. This legislation authorized formula grants to states to administer and operate programs that provide educational and support services to migrant children and youth. According to the U.S. Department of Education, the Migrant Education Program is intended to

➡ Establish a priority for the services for migratory children whose education has been interrupted during the school year and who are failing, or at risk of failing, to meet their state's content and performance standards

➻ Ensure that migrant children are provided with appropriate educational services (including support services such as health and social services) that address their special needs in a coordinated and efficient manner

➻ Require that states transfer student records and other data to other states and schools as students migrate

➻ Target the most recently mobile children, who experience the most disruption in schooling, by limiting the population counted to those who have moved within the previous three years

➻ Encourage the formation of consortia of states and other appropriate entities to reduce administrative and other costs for state migrant education programs (MEPs) and to make more funds available for direct services for children (U.S. Department of Education, 1999)

IDENTIFICATION AND RECRUITMENT OF STUDENTS

Identification and recruitment of migrant children, youth, and families are critical both to the success of the students involved and to the funding and consequent availability and the development of migrant programs. Because of this, the Migrant Education Program, the states that administer migrant education programs, and local migrant education programs all devote time, energy, and resources to identification and recruitment of migrant students.

The IASA mandates that states identify and recruit all eligible migrant children and youth in the state. It further describes the State Education Agency (SEA) responsibilities that identification and recruitment support. These include:

1. Determining the number of migrant children living in the state (Section 1304 (c)(7))
2. Determining the areas of the state to serve (Sections 1304 (b)(4) and (5))
3. Identifying and addressing the special educational needs of the migrant children, including preschool migrant children, through a comprehensive plan for needs assessment and service delivery (Section 1304(b)(1))
4. Serving migrant children according to the priority for services established in Section 1304 (d) which involves considering their relative educational needs and educational interruption

5. Determining the types of services that are most responsive to the special educational needs of the state's migrant children to allow them to meet the same challenging state content and performance standards all children are expected to meet (Sections 1304(b)(1) and (2)) (U.S. Department of Education, 1996a, 1)

Identifying and recruiting are perhaps the most difficult tasks required by the Migrant Education Program. The U.S. Department of Education suggests that local migrant education programs develop networks within their communities that support the identification and recruitment of eligible migrant students. The regulatory guidance the department provides for the Migrant Education Program includes the following examples of identification strategies. According to that guidance, states, school districts, and schools should

➽ Identify and map the locations of agricultural and commercial fishing areas. The U.S. Departments of Agriculture, Labor, and Commerce, and the State Office of Employment Security, can assist in many cases. Regional and local MEP staff may wish to contact individual growers and other agricultural and fishing employers.

➽ Obtain and maintain current information on the state's agricultural and fishing activities, and determine for each (1) areas of the state in which concentrations of migratory labor exist, and (2) peak employment periods. Ensure that recruitment staff are deployed in areas where concentrations of migrants are likely to reside.

➽ Coordinate with officials who administer the Women, Infants and Children (WIC), Migrant Health, Migrant Labor, Migrant Head Start, Community Service Block Grant programs, and other programs about the locations of migrant workers and families whom those programs serve. In some locations, recruiters canvas local churches, ESL classes, farmworker unions, legal aid agencies, and local businesses such as Laundromats, shopping malls, grocery stores, movie theaters, and restaurants to find migrant families.

➽ Locate and maintain current lists of migrant housing in each area of the state. State and federal Departments of Health (or Health and Human Services) and Labor may have lists of migrant camps.

•➔ Evaluate periodically the effectiveness of the state's identification efforts, and revise procedures as necessary. (U.S. Department of Education 1996a, 2)

The Migrant Education Program in Garden City, Kansas, U.S.D.
457, demonstrates how a team approach and collaboration supports
identification and recruitment. The Garden City migrant program has
developed a network that includes personnel from other school programs, local businesses and employers, community agencies, community organizations, and the local community college. The network and
the feelings of trust engendered by migrant program personnel within
the community form the basis of an effective system of identification
and recruitment.

This school district, in the southwestern corner of the state, currently serves approximately 2,300 migrant students, most of whom or
whose parents work in agribusiness such as meat and poultry processing. The families come from a variety of ethnic and cultural backgrounds;
many of them speak only Spanish or a Southeast Asian language.

In Garden City, the Migrant Education Program is administered
through the Office of Supplemental Programs of the school district. This
office is also responsible for other compensatory education programs
in the school district. These programs include the basic Title I program,
the English as a Second Language program, a Sustained Native Language (SNL) program, programs for homeless and refugee children, an
Even Start program, the Migrant Education Even Start program, a Pre-
kindergarten Four-Year Old program, and a Future Teachers program.

All the Migrant Education Program personnel are split-funded;
that is, they are funded partially through at least two of the programs administered by the Office of Supplemental Programs. Migrant Education
Program personnel thus work in at least two of the programs, which allows for collaboration and coordination across the programs. All the
supplemental programs staff are at least bilingual; collectively they can
communicate with nearly all the families in the school district. Two of
the staff members are former migrants themselves; they have firsthand
experience with being migrant and a special understanding of the needs
of and empathy for migrant families. Although each of the staff members has assigned duties within the Migrant Education Program, they
also work together as needed to meet the needs of the children and families they serve.

The Migrant Education Program has developed a network of organizations and agencies that assist in identification and recruitment.
These include IVP and ConAgra, the area's two largest employers; Em-

maus Place, the local food pantry; the Salvation Army; Mexican American Ministries; the area's health department; the Kansas Department of Social and Rehabilitation Services; churches in the community; community banks; the Finney County Extension Service; Catholic Ministries; and the Chamber of Commerce. The Migrant Education Program also has built relationships with local physicians, dentists, and eye doctors, as well as owners of rental properties and local businesses. Martin Segovia, the office's Family Literacy Liaison, grew up in Garden City; he recommends "knowing your community" as the most important way to identify and recruit migrant students.

Two of the Migrant Education Program staff members are officially recruiters, but all staff members are involved in identification and recruitment. The migrant program coordinator, for example, schedules regular visits to IVP and ConAgra to meet with new employees. During the meetings, she schedules appointments with the new employees for home visits to determine eligibility and complete the necessary paperwork, if they are eligible, to enroll their children in the Migrant Education Program, and to take the children to the clinic for health screenings. The recruiters make regular contact with community agencies and organizations, as well as regular visits to areas of the county where migrant families typically live. Many new families arrive in the community in the summer, and the recruiters report that sometimes they even go "door to door" then to find new families.

Part of the identification and recruitment process is building trust with migrant families; the families themselves then become part of the network for identification and recruitment. The Migrant Education Program staff work to build trust in many ways. Staff members provide translation for families who do not speak English, they help families find housing and access needed services in the community, and they have even paid for a month's rent for new or homeless families and taken families without transportation to purchase groceries. A current project with the migrant community is the development of a community garden. The Migrant Education Program in collaboration with the Finney County Extension Service, Catholic Ministries, and migrant families is developing a five-acre tract of land into a community garden. Migrant families will be able to tend their own garden plots and grow their own vegetables during the summer.

All these activities are aimed at building a strong network that supports identification and recruitment with the goal of providing appropriate educational services to every migrant child and family in the school district.

SCHOOLWIDE PROGRAMS

Schoolwide programs offer the opportunity to create exceptional learning environments as they serve children with a variety of educational needs. According to the guidance provided by the U.S. Department of Education for the Migrant Education Program, "schoolwide programs may use federal, state, and local funds *to upgrade a school's entire educational program,* provided that federal funds taken as a whole supplement state and local funds that would otherwise be sent at the school" (U.S. Department of Education 1996b, 1).

The guidance from the U.S. Department of Education provides examples of the potential of schoolwide programs. According to the guidance, schoolwide programs can

- Accelerate the curriculum to enable all students to meet high standards
- Encourage and facilitate collaboration and planning among regular classroom teachers, administrators, specialists, support staff, and parents
- Encourage innovation in instruction, use of time, staffing, and other resources
- Involve parents more centrally in planning, decision making, and instructional support roles
- Coordinate budgets from multiple sources
- Integrate and streamline pupil services, including diagnostic and counseling assistance as well as health services
- Consolidate and tailor professional development to a school's particular needs (U.S. Department of Education 1996b, 1)

Including migrant students in a schoolwide program does not allow a school to disregard the unique educational needs of migrant children and youth. When migrant students are included in schoolwide programs, the IASA requires that schools

- Consult with parents of migrant children or organizations representing those parents (or both)
- Address the identified needs of migrant children that result from the effects of their migrant lifestyle or are needed to permit children to participate effectively in school
- Document that service to address those needs have been provided (IASA 34CFR200.8(c)(3)(ii)(B)(1)) (U.S. Department of Education, 1996b)

As part of developing a schoolwide program, schools must conduct comprehensive assessments of the needs of the students who will be served in the program. When migrant students are served by the program, their particular needs must be assessed and included in the program planning.

According to the U.S. Department of Education, schoolwide programs that serve migrant students can be effective in meeting the needs of those students by:

- Providing an "enrichment" rather than a "deficit" model of instruction
- Validating migrant students' language and culture, including their migrant experiences
- Supporting the aspirations of migrant students and providing them with role models from the local community
- Implementing bilingual curricula and programs, employing bilingual staff, and providing for the full involvement of the parents of migrant children
- Maintaining and transferring students' education and health records (U.S. Department of Education 1996b, 2, 3)

A schoolwide program identified by the U.S. Department of Education as exemplifying the vision these components set for schoolwide programs that serve migrant students is the Glassbrook Elementary School in Hayward, California. Since the school was identified in 1994 as "a promising schoolwide program," Glassbrook Elementary School has continued to develop the schoolwide program and adapt it to meet the needs of all the children in the school.

Glassbrook Elementary School serves children in preschool through third grade. It has a population that is both culturally diverse— more than two-thirds of the students are Hispanic, Afghan, African American, Asian, Filipino, or Indian/Pakistani—and economically disadvantaged. Because the school population has high rates of poverty, nearly all the students qualify for free or reduced-price lunches. The mobility rate of students at the school is between 60 and 70 percent, and many of the students in the school are migrant.

The staff of Glassbrook Elementary School began planning for its multicultural and multilingual schoolwide program in 1990; the program has been in operation since the 1992–1993 school year. The planning goal for the schoolwide program was building consensus among stakeholders about how best to raise the level of student achievement, the result being that the school's bilingual program was expanded to encompass the entire curriculum.

More than half the children in the school come from homes where a language other than English is spoken; most of those children have Spanish as their first language. Since California's Proposition 227 restricted the language of classroom instruction to English and the provision of bilingual support to only one year, Glassbrook Elementary School parents sought waivers for their children. The waivers were supported by the school district, and all students at the school participate in the school's dual-language program. According to a description of the school by the U.S. Department of Education,

> Spanish-speaking teachers and . . . language development specialists conduct the bilingual education for both English-language students and Spanish-speaking students. Using a "staggered" activity schedule, teachers alternate the language of instruction in a consistent pattern each day, offering core subjects in both English and Spanish and relying on bilingual learning centers and students' writing. (U.S. Department of Education 1994, 2)

Curriculum and instruction at Glassbrook is theme-based and project-oriented. Teachers and other school personnel have designed thematic instruction to integrate the traditional curriculum areas in content that is meaningful and relevant to the children's diversity. Social studies is the framework around which other core areas of the curriculum are organized; themes highlight cultural or ethnic backgrounds and knowledge of the students. Literature used at the school is multicultural, and instructional and curricular materials have been translated into students' first languages to ensure access for all students. In addition, teachers use a variety of inclusive instructional strategies, including "peer coaching, cooperative learning, and learning through projects and experiments" (U.S. Department of Education 1994, 1). The school and classroom environment at the school is characterized by "respect, tolerance, and an appreciation for cultural diversity" (U.S. Department of Education 1994, 1).

Glassbrook has continued to assess the needs of its students and revise or adjust the program to meet the identified needs of the students. Evidence of the school's focus on meeting the children's needs is the recent expansion of the school's preschool program. Glassbrook has had a Head Start program for several years, but the language of instruction in that program is English. To ensure that children whose first language is Spanish have a preschool experience, Glassbrook recently began a preschool program in Spanish.

Parents have been involved in Glassbrook's schoolwide program since the beginning of the planning. Since then, parents have played an active role in the school's classrooms. The school also offers several parent workshops each year, as well as English as a Second Language (ESL) classes for parents.

A congressionally mandated study of how the needs of migrant students were being met in schoolwide programs found that in the 1996–1997 school year, about 28 percent of migrant children were served in schoolwide programs (Siler et al. 1999, 1). There were significantly more schools whose schoolwide programs served migrant students in states that have the largest populations of migrant students, such as Texas, California, and Florida.

INTERSTATE AND BINATIONAL COORDINATION AND COLLABORATION

According to the regulatory guidance for the Migrant Education Program:

> the reauthorized ESEA places great emphasis on collaboration among states. All states are encouraged to collaborate in order to provide effective services to migrant children, especially states with smaller grants under the MEP. . . . The secretary [of Education] is directed to approve any SEA consortium proposal that (1) reduces MEP administrative costs or program function costs . . . and (2) increases the amount of MEP funds available for direct services to migrant children that add substantially to the educational attainment or welfare of those children. . . . (Migrant Education Program 1995)

The legislation that authorizes the Migrant Education Program encourages states and school districts to establish relationships that lower the administrative costs of the Migrant Education Program so that larger proportions of the program's funding are used in direct service to migrant children.

Some states have entered into consortium agreements that enhance services provided to migrant students. These consortia operate for several purposes. Some of them facilitate administration of programs across states. One such consortium, CAIR, exists to support the identification and recruitment of migrant students. The Upper Midwest Consortium provides materials and professional development for migrant education programs in the states in the consortium. Others, such as the East Atlantic-Caribbean Consortium, have worked toward more effective and efficient transfer of student records.

CAIR

The Consortium Agreement, Identification and Recruitment, or CAIR, was organized to assist states in their efforts to identify and recruit migrant students. CAIR focuses its efforts on developing and enhancing identification and recruitment practices in and communication between its partner states. Partner states in this consortium are Alabama, Arkansas, Colorado, Connecticut, Florida, Illinois, Iowa, Kansas, Maine, Maryland, Missouri, Nebraska, New Hampshire, New York, North Carolina, Oklahoma, Pennsylvania, South Carolina, Tennessee, Texas, Vermont, Virginia, West Virginia, and Wyoming. Many of the migrant workers in these states work for such agribusinesses as meat and poultry producers. CAIR has worked to develop alliances with these agribusinesses to support the identification and recruitment of migrant students and their families. In addition to facilitating and supporting networks for identification and recruitment, CAIR has also sponsored professional development for migrant education personnel from its member states (CAIR 1999).

The Upper Midwest Consortium

The Upper Midwest Consortium includes Iowa, Minnesota, North Dakota, and South Dakota; the consortium was formed to support instruction in migrant education programs in those states. Schools there that serve the children of migrant workers have access to the Minnesota Migrant Education Resource Center (MMERC) services at no cost. MMERC has an extensive collection of educational materials that are available to schools and migrant education programs in the consortium states. The collection includes audiovisual materials; books, many of which are bilingual or in Spanish; games and manipulatives for hands-on learning; thematic multimedia unit boxes; teacher and parent reference materials; and materials appropriate for ESL. In addition to providing materials that support instruction in migrant education programs, the MMERC has a staff of education professionals who conduct teacher workshops, inservices, or site visits to meet specific district needs or topics for schools and migrant programs in the member states. Other services that MMERC provides include facilitating workshops or inservices for migrant parents, publishing a migrant education newsletter, "el informe," and supporting distance learning and secondary summer curriculum (MMERC 2001).

East Atlantic-Caribbean Consortium

The East Atlantic-Caribbean Consortium was formed to develop a database management system to maintain and transfer migrant student records when the MSRTS ceased its operations. Members of the consortium include Maryland, Connecticut, Pennsylvania, and the Commonwealth of Puerto Rico. The East Atlantic-Caribbean Consortium, which has Pennsylvania as the lead state, working together, realized "tremendous savings of money, time, and effort for all the states involved" (East Atlantic-Caribbean Consortium 1999).

These, as well as several other consortia, serve to provide efficiency of scale, especially for small states, in administration of migrant education programs at the level of SEAs.

INTERSTATE, INTRASTATE, AND INTERAGENCY COORDINATION

The Migrant Education Program also encourages coordination between and among states, school districts, and schools to address the educational discontinuity that migrant children and youth face as they move. In particular, these interstate, intrastate, and interagency coordination efforts are intended to serve as a safety net for migrant children and families.

The Office of Migrant Education supports a toll-free telephone number that migrant parents can use to obtain information about the nearest migrant programs available to them when they move. States, school districts, and schools have developed many coordinated and collaborative programs to assist migrant students.

Teacher exchange is one way that states and schools provide continuity of teaching and learning. Summer migrant programs often hire teachers from students' home-base schools who then travel with the students and work with them in summer programs along their travel routes. The Pennsylvania Migrant Program, for example,

> employs teachers from different parts of Mexico, Florida, Texas, and Puerto Rico in various sites across the state each summer. The teachers bring a sense of familiarity and continuity to the migrant children's summer, inservice local migrant program and school district staff on the educational systems in Puerto Rico and Mexico, and promote connections across programs offered in different states so as to reduce the fragmentation that occurs when a child's education is interrupted. (Migrant Education Program 1995, 2)

Other states use similar teacher exchanges to provide continuity for the students they serve in summer migrant programs.

Another example of coordination designed to provide educational continuity for migrant students is Project SMART (Summer Migrants Access Resources Through Technology). Project SMART is a distance learning program that originated in San Antonio, Texas, in 1992, and is national in scope. Project SMART reaches migrant students in summer programs across Texas and in other states to which Texas students migrate. The design of Project SMART is flexible, allowing for schools to participate either through home- or center-based programs. Project SMART is based on a series of televised lessons that can be accessed live and interactive, live but not interactive, delayed, or videotaped.

Project SMART televises lessons in five instructional strands for five levels of schooling: preschool, early elementary grades, upper elementary grades, middle school, and high school. Teachers who teach the lessons are experienced and skilled in working with migrant students and in television instruction. Local teachers in summer migrant programs are expected to serve as facilitators and co-teachers as they provide follow up or extend the lessons of Project SMART, and also as assessors and monitors of student progress. Project SMART provides follow-up activities to the lessons, and local teachers participate in professional development designed to help them facilitate and build on the lessons with their students.

This project offers high school students the opportunity for credit accrual through live or videotaped courses in American Government, Economics, Informal Geometry A, World Geography A and B, Algebra IA, Creative Writing, Mathematics of Money A, and Pre-Algebra A and B. Migrant students can also prepare for the TAAS (Texas Assessment of Academic Skills, the state assessment) through TAAS Reading Preparation or TAAS Math Preparation.

Project SMART lessons are provided in Spanish and English to be accessible and relevant to students. Lessons are also designed to be authentic to and connect with the life experiences of migrant students. Instructional materials used in the lessons are readily available to teachers and students (Wisconsin Department of Public Instruction 2000).

Another example of coordination across states that supports migrant student learning can be seen in the PASS (Portable Assisted Study Sequence) described in Chapter 3. The PASS courses provide continuity of curriculum for students as they move from school to school. Course content in the PASS program has been developed and is continuously revised in accordance with national standards. The course content is also examined to ensure that it meets the state content and performance standards for which students will be held accountable in their home states. All the states that use PASS have agreed to accept credits that students accrue through the program.

The efforts to transfer students' records described in Chapter 3 are also examples of coordination and collaboration designed to break down the bureaucratic barriers students face as they migrate across the country. Besides the efforts to transfer these records electronically, there have been less sophisticated (but no less successful) records exchanges. Several states have worked to help parents and teachers understand the importance of the timely transfer of records. Texas, for example, has involved parents in the records transfer process. They have provided special blue tote bags in which parents transport copies of their children's educational and health records and present when they enroll their children in new schools. Under this very simple system, the children's records are available immediately at the new school, and students can be placed appropriately and receive the services they need.

TECHNOLOGY IN MIGRANT EDUCATION

Although individual schools and classrooms that serve migrant children and youth may be using technology, the Office of Migrant Education has supported a series of larger technology projects that are exploring and demonstrating ways that technology-based learning can be used to address the particular needs of migrant students. Preliminary evaluations of the five initial technology projects point to some tentative positive outcomes:

- The technology projects are increasing migrant students' access to technology and proficiency at using technology.
- Teachers engaged in the projects are becoming more adept at using technology as a teaching tool and are making both a personal and professional commitment to learning with their children.
- Technology provides a flexible, individualized method of providing instructional content, which is particularly valuable for students who move.
- The technology is a means of communicating with the home-base school and of developing a spirit of community and camaraderie among students who are far from home.
- Students become self-learners; the computer motivates them to engage in learning and enhances their self-image.
- Projects are seeing a paradigm shift from the "poor pitiful kid" syndrome to a view of migrant students as engaged in powerful, cutting-edge instructional strategies that can

drive instruction for other children. (Office of Migrant Education 2000, 1, 2)

The Office of Migrant Education awarded grants originally to five technology projects. They expanded the grant program to include an additional six technology projects in the fall of 2000.

The five original technology projects funded by the Migrant Education Program are Project MECHA, ★Estrella, InTIME, KMTP, and Anchor School. Each of the projects involves a variety of community, technology, and educational partners who contribute support and expertise to the project. A short description of each project is provided here. More information about these programs is available at the programs' Web sites, listed in Chapter 8.

Project MECHA stands for Migrant Education Consortium for Higher Achievement. This project, centered in Florida, supports migrant students in grades three through twelve who travel between Florida and Georgia, South Carolina, North Carolina, and Pennsylvania, through the use of Web-TV. Students in MECHA each have an individualized lesson plan (ILP) that extends their academic and health records to include demographic information, placement and skill levels, health concerns, and teacher comments and recommendations. Because these ILPs are online, teachers in receiving states can access them. MECHA facilitates communication between teachers in Florida and students' receiving teachers. Students in the MECHA project have Web-TV devices that allow them access to e-mail and the Internet; this access allows them to communicate with their home-base schools in Florida. Students in MECHA also are provided with online mentors.

★Estrella (Encouraging Student Through Technology to Reach High Expectations In Learning, Lifeskills, and Achievement) was designed by migrant educators from Illinois, Texas, Montana, and New York with the goal of increasing the high school graduation rate and preparing students for the possibility of postsecondary education. ★Estrella provides each student with a laptop computer, software, and access to the Internet so they can complete coursework begun in Texas while they are traveling. A coordinator, based in Texas, regularly communicates with students and oversees technology maintenance. High school counselors and teachers in students' home-base and receiving schools are involved in ★Estrella, approving courses students take online and participating in professional development in the use of technology for learning. Students are assigned cyber mentors, college students who communicate with the students online; an annual conference on a university campus allows the high school and college students to meet face-to-face and also gives the high school students a taste of college life. ★Estrella is described in more detail in Chapter 5.

InTIME (Integrating Technology Into Migrant Education) is a project that has explored various technology solutions to support the more than 23,000 students who migrate within the state of Oregon. The project brings together a large menu of components that include Computer Adaptive Testing; a Spanish-language placement system for mathematics; instructional uses of software and the Internet; wireless networked collaborative note taking; NovaNET online secondary courses; Mathemagica, which is homework support via public television for middle school students; CIM summer school, which provides intensive support for developing and improving skill in writing; Ready to Learn, Oregon Public Broadcasting workshops for young children and their families; OMSIS, the statewide student record computer system; and a Web site that describes all the activities available through the InTIME project. The InTIME Web site also includes a searchable database of social services that allows families to find sources of needed services.

The Kentucky Migrant Technology Project (KMTP) has several goals, among them improving migrant student achievement, increasing comfort levels and skills of teachers and students in using technology, and decreasing the migrant student dropout rate. The project is using technology to provide a high-quality curriculum that is motivational and multimedia, as well as personally relevant, to the migrant student population in Kentucky. Students in the project are provided with Personal Digital Assistants to use in school and at home.

The Anchor School project, based in Collier County, Florida, combines technology and a human team that travels with the migrant students as they migrate within and between states in the Southeast United States. The Anchor project partners with NASA and Gargiulo, one of the largest employers of migrant farmworkers in the country. The project has created a database that supports correlation of teaching materials with state standards in Florida, North Carolina, South Carolina, and Tennessee. A variety of technologies are used to support communication among teachers and other education program personnel, families, and students.

Technology is a vehicle that can support high-quality distance learning for migrant children and families. It can also be a medium for professional development for teachers; resources for teachers, students, and parents; and opportunities for learning for all members of a learning community. Chapter 6 provides a description of how technology is being used in one Colorado Board of Cooperative Education Services (BOCES) to bring a wide variety of compensatory education programs together in support of migrant education, and to level the playing field by providing access to technology to migrant families.

ADULT EDUCATION AND FAMILY LITERACY PROGRAMS

Research has long shown that educational success is an intergenerational process. There is a strong correlation between the level of parents' education and the academic achievement of their children. The Migrant Education Program includes the Migrant Education Even Start program (MEES) for the very purpose of helping migrant parents to access educational opportunities for themselves. At the same time, the MEES program is intended to support parents as their children's first teacher, to advocate for their children by participating actively in their schooling, and to develop effective parenting skills.

Many communities have also offered other kinds of adult education programs to migrant families. These programs help migrant adults develop literacy in both English and Spanish, earn high school diplomas or GEDs (general equivalency diplomas), and function in a culture that is foreign to them.

One English-language adult education program involved teachers playing traditional games such as Bingo and UNO with migrant adults at their camps and homes after their evening meal. A teacher in this Pennsylvania program kept a journal about her experiences with the students. Her entries demonstrate that her involvement with the students went beyond the curriculum to include concern for her students as people. This journal entry shows how she used the students' interests to develop and extend their English and literacy lessons.

> September 13—Seneca Castle
> A delightful evening! I brought the tape recorder again. . . . We recorded Max, Moises, and Samuel in dialogues of the questions and answers we had practiced. They enjoyed it. But, since their English is so limited, we soon ran out of conversation to record. Then—serendipity . . . I had an idea. I didn't know if it would work or cause me to make a fool of myself. In my desperation to use the recorder more, I turned to singing. None of my students wanted to be recorded singing a Spanish song, so . . . I taught them "Row, Row, Row Your Boat." They loved it! (Much to my relief and pleasure.) So we practiced and recorded this little American ditty for the rest of the evening. We brought out the apple juice and our hilarity and enjoyment attracted Benito, Domingo, Israel and Fran-

cisco, and Miguel came back, too. We got him on tape, introducing our song. It was fun and relaxing. In this kind of setting my students are sometimes inclined to risk a little English conversation: I was pleased when Samuel, for example, asked me how many years I had been coming out to camp, and where I lived. (Zimmer 1996, 14)

Other programs help migrant families gain cultural knowledge that will help them navigate the legal system in the United States. One such program, in Eagle County in Colorado, is operated by the court. Through this program, the court offers recent migrants and immigrants "a three-hour crash course on the legal and cultural do's and don'ts of life in the U.S." as an alternative sentence. The course is designed to help these migrants and immigrants understand such concepts as "bail bonds, warrants, and plea bargains." The instructors also teach basic survival skills and suggest that course participants work to become part of the community and learn English (Woodbury 2000, 8).

BILINGUAL AND ESL PROGRAMS

Because many migrant families speak languages other than English at home, bilingual education is a key factor in the success of migrant children, youth, and families in education programs. Effective bilingual and ESL programs use a variety of formats to meet the needs of the students in them. According to Krashen, the best bilingual education programs include ESL instruction, sheltered subject matter teaching, and instruction in students' first languages (Krashen 1997, 1).

> Non-English speaking children initially receive core instruction in the primary language along with ESL instruction. As children grow more proficient in English, they learn subjects using more contextualized language (e.g., math and science) in sheltered classes taught in English, and eventually in mainstream classes. In this way, the sheltered classes function as a bridge between instruction in the first language and in the mainstream. In advanced levels, the only subjects done in the first language are those demanding the most abstract use of language (social studies and language arts). Once full mainstreaming is complete, advanced first language development is available as an option. *Gradual exit plans,* such as these, avoid problems associated with exiting children too early (before the English they encounter is comprehensible) and provide instruction in the first language where it is more needed. These plans also allow children to have the advantages of advanced first language development. (Krashen 1997, 1)

Effective programs for English-language learners, then, are not only planned based on research. They also take into account information about the progress of each student.

The Center for Research on Education, Diversity & Excellence (CREDE) has established five standards for effective teaching and learning from extensive review of the research on teaching and learning. The standards are:

1. Joint productive activity: Teacher and students producing together
2. Language development: Developing language scross the curriculum
3. Making meaning: Connecting school to students' lives
4. Cognitive challenge: Teaching complex thinking
5. Instructional conversation: Teaching through conversation (Echevarria 1998, 1)

"For students whose educational success is at risk due to factors like poverty or language differences," Echevarria argues, "the Standards are vital" (Echevarria 1998, 1). CREDE has also investigated a wide range of methods and strategies for teaching language to minority students. The second of the standards, which addresses language development, is particularly important for language minority students. It sets the expectation that language can and should be developed as a key element of the entire school curriculum. According to CREDE, four teaching practices are critical to students' language development, regardless of age or school level. Teachers should (1) understand the language needs of students, (2) explicitly plan to meet those needs, (3) deliver instruction, and (4) assess students' comprehension (Echevarria 1998, 1; Echevarria and Goldenberg 1999, 1).

Robert Bahruth's classroom in a border district in Texas is one example of how the four teaching practices identified by CREDE support both language learning and learning in other areas of the curriculum. Instruction in Bahruth's classroom included ESL instruction, sheltered subject matter teaching, and instruction in the students' first language.

Robert Bahruth worked with bilingual migrant students in a Texas school beginning in 1983. He found that even when the migrant students in his classroom could speak English well enough to carry on a conversation, they often did not have adequate academic language skills, the language necessary to be successful in the academic work expected in most classrooms. Bahruth and his co-authors, Curtis W. Hayes and Carolyn Kessler, describe his work with bilingual migrant students in a school in a small town in south Texas in their book, *Literacy con Cariño*. Many students in Bahruth's fifth-grade class began the year as non-readers and nonwriters; all the students had achievement levels far below their assigned grade level. Bahruth's instructional program met all the standards identified by CREDE. Most important for these language minority students, Bahruth focused with his students on developing language skills and literacy in activities that were relevant and authentic to the students' life experiences throughout the curriculum.

By the end of the school year with Bahruth, all the students were reading and writing; samples of their work included in the book demonstrate their increasing proficiency in reading and writing English, as well as in their learning throughout the curriculum. The success of his students in raising their levels of English-language literacy led Bahruth to synthesize what he and his co-authors call "key pedagogical adjustments that are essential" to the students' educational success and that offer further guidance on implementing the CREDE standards with English-language learners. The elements of the list below, adapted from Bahruth's "key pedagogical adjustments," align with the research on effective literacy instruction in general:

- Active, interactive classrooms where talking about the learning is encouraged
- The use of language "as a tool for learning about their [the students'] world"
- A focus on learning rather than on teaching, and on appreciating and building on students' "experiences and linguistic and cultural foundations"
- Integrated and interesting curriculum, and assessment that provides information to help teachers guide students in their learning
- Timely nudges from teachers
- Developmental appropriateness—the understanding that students' learning progresses on individual paths and at individual rates
- Teachers who are "intellectually engaged and reflective practitioners" (Hayes, Bahruth, and Kessler 1998, 149–153)

These key pedagogical adjustments are appropriate not only for bilingual education but for creating educational programs and classrooms where migrant children and youth have real opportunities to learn and be successful.

Addressing the language needs of middle school and high school students who arrive in U.S. schools with little or no English is often more difficult than addressing the language needs of younger children. Secondary students sometimes arrive with little academic preparation overall; language then becomes only a small part of the challenge of helping these youth to be successful in middle and high school classrooms. Some schools have addressed this issue by developing newcomer programs "that serve these students through a program of intensive language development and academic and cultural orientation, for a limited period of time (usually from 6–18 months), before placing them in the regular school language support and academic programs" (Short 1998, 1).

Newcomer programs have different designs and formats, but they all serve the purpose of helping students to develop the language and academic skills necessary to be prepared to enter a mainstream secondary education program with "regular language support" (Short 1998, 1).

A study of newcomer programs found that a typical newcomer program operates as a school within a school, as a full day, or, in some cases, a half-day program. Besides English-language instruction, students are also provided with content area instruction. "Because a large number of the students [eligible for newcomer programs] have limited education backgrounds, many of the content classes are designed to help students learn the basic foundations of core subjects" (Short 1998, 2). Some newcomer programs allow students to participate for a specific amount of time; at the end of that period, generally a school year, students move from the newcomer program to a regular ESL or bilingual program. More flexible newcomer programs base the decision about when to exit on students' language proficiency and their readiness to participate in mainstream programs.

According to Short's review, most newcomer programs help students make the transition from the program. These transition activities may include taking students on tours of the school and providing them with opportunities to visit regular classes and to meet guidance counselors. Many of the programs also provide follow-up services in the form of mentoring and tutoring after the students have left the newcomer program (Short 1998, 2).

BINATIONAL PROGRAMS AND COLLABORATION

Because so many migrant children and youth cross the U.S.-Mexico border each year as part of their migration, the notion of binational cooperation and collaboration is an important one. Several binational programs have been instituted to address the educational discontinuity that these children and youth experience. These programs, at all levels from the federal level in both countries to the classroom level, all depend at least in part on high levels of understanding of the educational process in both countries.

The Mexican government officials have taken an active role in binational efforts because they "consider the Mexican nation as a geopolitical entity that stretches beyond its geographical limits" (Secretaria de Relaciones Exteriores n.d., 3). One of the binational programs that serves Mexican citizens and Mexican Americans in the United States is the *Programa para las Comunidades Mexicanas en el Extranjero* (the Program for Mexican Communities Abroad). This program, sponsored by the Mexican State Department, includes several components to help Mexican communities in the United States meet the educational needs of Mexican citizens and Mexican Americans. These components include teacher exchanges between the United States and Mexico, adult education, the Binational Transfer Document, immersion courses for bilingual teachers in the United States, the donation of Mexican textbooks, and youth activities designed to help children and young people understand their Mexican heritage. The programs are administered in the United States by a network of Mexican Cultural and Educational Institutes.

The *Instituto Mexicano de Cultura y Educación de Chicago* (Mexican Cultural and Educational Institute of Chicago) is one of the organizations the Mexican government sponsors in the United States that implements the Program for Mexican Communities Abroad. The Mexican Cultural and Educational Institute of Chicago serves the large and growing population of Mexican Americans and Mexican citizens living in Chicago. This institute in Chicago has been in operation for eight years, according to Nora Oranday, the institute's media and educational coordinator.

The Mexican Cultural and Educational Institute of Chicago is involved in several educational programs. These include the provision of Mexican textbooks to schools and Mexican and Mexican American families, a teacher exchange between the United States and Mexico in collaboration with the Illinois State Board of Education, and assisting families with Binational Transfer Documents. The institute also sponsors activities aimed at helping Mexican citizens in Chicago and Mexican Americans understand their Mexican heritage and culture and negotiate the culture and resources of Chicago.

Although the staff of the institute is small, Ms. Oranday described the institute's efforts to seek collaborations and alliances with other organizations; their goal is to maximize their resources so that they can extend their services to as many people as possible. Currently, the Mexican Cultural and Educational Institute of Chicago is a partner in a pilot distance learning project with two high schools in Chicago, Benito Juarez High School and the West Side Technical Institute, and the Institute for Latino Progress. Through funding from UNESCO, high school classes from Mexico are broadcast via satellite television to the high schools. The broadcasts, which include eight cultural channels, as well as tutoring, ESL, and computers, are available to high school students and adults. Participation in the program allows students to continue their Mexican high school educations. For adults, the program offers the Mexican equivalent of a GED; educators come from Mexico to administer the test required for the diploma. Ms. Oranday reported that several additional schools are interested in participating in the program, and that as additional resources become available, more schools will be added to the project.

MIGRANT HEALTH CARE

The U.S. Department of Health and Human Services administers a network of health centers that are aimed at making health care services accessible to migrant and seasonal farmworkers. Although these health centers are not funded by migrant education programs, the services offered by these health centers are vital to migrant students' success in school. According to the Catalog of Federal Domestic Assistance (2000, 4), in fiscal year 1999, approximately 122 migrant health projects were funded. The objectives for these projects are "to support the development and operation of Health Centers and Migrant health programs which provide primary health care services, supplemental health services, technical assistance and environmental health services, which are accessible to migrant and seasonal agricultural farmworkers and their families as they work and move" (Catalog of Federal Domestic Assistance 2000, 1). The service provided through these projects has the potential for great impact on migrant children and their families.

One such project, in operation since 1988, is in St. Lucie County, Florida. St. Lucie County, on the east coast of the state, has a large migrant community. According to the National Health Service Corps, "the health care situation in St. Lucie County was dismal," as evidenced by "more than 230 cases of low to very low birth weights . . . reported in 1988" (National Health Service Corps 2000, 1). This high incidence of low birth weight babies has a potential impact on education; children with low birth weight have a higher likelihood of developing learning problems.

In 1988, before the initiation of this migrant health care project, one pediatrician and three obstetricians staffed the community hospital. They were burdened with an overactive emergency room and lacked the time to provide primary health care to the community, specifically the preventive medicine and pre-natal care so crucial for pregnant mothers. . . . To make matters worse, the community hospital was not technically equipped to handle newborns who required incubation upon delivery. These children required transfer to tertiary care centers over 100 miles away." (National Health Service Corps 2000, 1)

In addition, between one-half and one-third of children in the county were not immunized, and there were many cases of tuberculosis, syphilis, and AIDS.

In 1988, three pediatricians and one obstetrician from the National Health Service Corps arrived in St. Lucie County. They provided the well-child care and pre-natal counseling that the four physicians practicing there had been too pressed for time to implement. According to one of the National Health Service Corps physicians, "These residents were thrilled to finally be able to say that they had a family doctor all their own; word spread like wildfire that there were physicians willing to be there day and night, to know them, to care for them, on a continuous basis" (National Health Service Corps 2000, 2).

The National Health Service Corps reports that there has been a dramatic drop in emergency room visits, and overall an "influx of health in St. Lucie County." The National Health Service Corps physician commented that "people believed for a long time that providing primary health care to poor communities still wouldn't solve the problem because the parents wouldn't take advantage of the care. What happened in St. Lucie's [sic] County confirms my assumptions that this is utterly untrue. If you provide care, people will use it" (National Health Service Corps 2000, 2).

Some organizations are involved in providing direct health care services to migrant families, in providing health care education to migrant families, and in providing support services to health care providers who serve migrant families. These include the Migrant Health Centers, the National Center for Farmworker Health, Inc., and the Migrant Clinicians Network. Migrant Health Centers offer direct health care services, as well as referrals to other health care providers, to migrant farmworkers and their families. The National Center for Farmworker Health conducts research about migrant health issues, develops and provides educational materials for health care professionals to use with migrant farmworkers and their families, and generally works as an advocate to improve health care services for migrants. The National Center assists migrants with accessing appropriate health care services through its toll-free telephone health care referral service, as well as translation services where necessary to support access to health care and health care information. The Migrant Clinicians Network is engaged in research on migrant health care issues and also develops health care education materials for migrants. To ensure the continuity of appropriate health care services, the network maintains a national and international database and patient tracking for migrant patients suffering from diabetes and tuberculosis.

The Migrant Education Program and its various components, other federally funded compensatory education programs, and such support services as the health care services described above, all seek to break down the barriers to educational success experienced by migrant families and their children. For some migrant families, these services do provide a safety net that helps them and their children to complete high school and postsecondary education and to have opportunities for employment outside of migrant farmwork. But some migrant families still slip through that safety net, and families with few or no options for other employment continue to join the ranks of migrant farmworkers.

In 1992, the National Association of State Directors of Migrant Education (NASDME) challenged the U.S. Department of Education, State Education Agencies, school districts, and schools to rethink how they served migrant children and youth. NASDME asked schools to design programs that break down the barriers to education that migrant children and youth face and help them to reach the National Education Goals (NASDME 1992). In 1994, the reauthorization of the Migrant Education Program in the Improving America's Schools Act drew on that challenge in its mandate to schools to design programs that would help migrant students meet the same high standards set for all children in their states. In 2001, there are still too many migrant students who are not graduating from high school or being prepared to enroll in postsecondary education. There are too many schools that have not risen to the challenge to ensure high levels of academic achievement for all migrant children and youth. The challenge remains.

REFERENCES

Catalog of Federal Domestic Assistance. 93.246: *Health Care Grants for Migrant and Seasonal Farmworkers, 2000.* Available: http://aspe.os.dhhs.gov/cfda/p93246.htm#134

Consortium Agreement, Identification and Recruitment (CAIR). 1999. Available: http://104.233.60.2/cair/

East Atlantic-Caribbean Consortium: Background and Rationale. 1999. Available: http://www.cciu.org/OtherHoePages/PAMIgrantEd/EACCRationale. html

Echevarria, J. *Teaching Language Minority Students in Elementary School. Research Brief #1.* Santa Cruz, CA: Center for Research on Education, Diversity & Research, University of California, 1998.

Echevarria, J., and C. Goldenberg. *Teaching Secondary Language Minority Students. Research Brief #4.* Santa Cruz, CA: Center for Research on Education, Diversity & Research, University of California, 1999.

Hayes, C. W., R. Bahruth, and C. Kessler. *Literacy con Cariño; A Story of Migrant Children's Success.* (New Edition). Portsmouth, NH: Heinmann, 1998.

Krashen, S. "Why Bilingual Education?" *ERIC Digest.* Charleston, WV: Clearinghouse on Rural Education and Small Schools, 1997.

Migrant Education Program. *Preliminary Guidance for Migrant Education Program, Title I, Part C Public Law 103–382: Interstate, Intrastate, and Interagency Coordination.* Washington, DC: Migrant Education Program, 1995. (Available: http://www.ed.gov/offices/OESE/MEP/PrelimGuide/pt1c.html)

Minnesota Migrant Education Resource Center (MMERC). 2001. Available: http://web.hamline.edu/graduate/centers/mmerc/

National Association of State Directors of Migrant Education (NASDME). *Giving Migrant Students an Opportunity to Learn.* Sunnyside, WA: National Association of Migrant Educators, 1994.

National Health Service Corps. *NHSC Profile: St. Lucie County, Florida,* 2000. Available: http://www.bphc.hrsa.dhhs.gov/nhsc/Pages/about_njsc/3D4a_FL.htm

Office of Migrant Education. *Migrant Education Technology Grants.* Washington, DC: Office of Migrant Education, 2000. Available: http://www.ed.gov/offices/ OESE/MEP/nl1lead.html

Pilar. "A Street Kids Guide." *Estupendas.* Newsletter of the ★Estrella project (1999): 11.

Secretaria de Relaciones Exteriores. *Programa para las Comunidades Mexicana en el Extranjero (The Program for Mexican Communities Abroad).* Morales, Mexico: Author, n.d.

Short, D. J. "Secondary Newcomer Programs: Helping Recent Immigrants Prepare for School Success." *ERIC Digest.* Washington, DC: ERIC Clearinghouse on Languages and Linguistics, Center for Applied Linguistics, 1998.

———. Executive Summary. *Meeting the Needs of Migrant Students in Schoolwide Programs: Technical Report of the Congressionally Mandated Study of Migrant Student Participation in Schoolwide Programs.* Rockville, MD: Westat, 1999.

U.S. Department of Education. "Building on What Students Know." *Implementing Schoolwide Projects.* Washington, DC: U.S. Department of Education, 1994. Available: http:// www.ed.gov/pubs/SchlProj/prof6.html

———. "Identification and Recruitment." Preliminary Guidance for Migrant Education Program, Title I, Part C Public Law 103–382, 1996a.

———. "Serving Migrant Children in Schoolwide Programs." Preliminary Guidance for Migrant Education Program, Title I, Part C Public Law 103–382, 1996b. Available: http://www.ed.gov/ofices/OESE/MEP/PrelimGuide/pt3a.html

———. *Promising Results, Continuing Challenges: Final Report of the National Assessment of Title I.* Washington, DC: U.S. Department of Education, 1999.

Wisconsin Department of Public Instruction. *Migrant Education Program: Project SMART,* 2000. Available: http://www.dpi.state.wi.us/dpi/

Woodbury, R. "A Class for Strangers in a Strange Land." *Time* 155, no. 18 (1 May 2000): 8.

Zimmer, K. *Teaching in a Migrant Camp: 1994–1995 Journal Notes.* Geneseo, NY: BOCES Geneseo Migrant Center, 1996. (ERIC Document Reproduction Service No. 415038)

Chapter Five

❧ Exemplary and Innovative Migrant Education Programs

In 1994, the National Association of State Directors of Migrant Education (NASDME) published a set of Opportunity-to-Learn Standards that underscore the equity they had addressed earlier in their response to the National Education Goals. According to the document, the standards were designed to

- ❧ highlight the special considerations to take into account regarding the education of migrant children
- ❧ provide a systematic way of responding to the diverse needs of migrant children in the United States
- ❧ offer insights into the very real struggles arising from the demanding, mobile lifestyle of migrant children
- ❧ assist schools, districts, and states in strategically planning reform strategies with the education of all children in mind (NASDME 1994, 1)

The five standards are based on the assumption that all children can learn and be successful if schools, school districts, and states understand the issues facing migrant children and youth and actively plan to address those issues. Equal access to the same educational programs that are provided for all students is not enough to ensure equal learning outcomes for migrant students. Schools, school districts, and states must make "a commitment . . . to make alternative educational strategies available that are specifically targeted to migrant students. . . . It will require 'more than equal' services and commitment to ensure that migrant students realize equity in the attainment of performance standards set for all students" (NASDME 1994, 6).

The standards delineate a framework for designing educational programs for migrant children and youth that could ensure equity of outcomes for migrant students.

Opportunity-to Learn-Standards
Standard 1: Equitable Access to Education Opportunities
    A: Access to equitable resources and financing among schools, districts, and states
    B. Access to technology
    C. Access to linguistically appropriate instruction
    D. Access to developmentally appropriate early childhood education programs
    E. Access to challenging curriculum and quality instruction
    F. Accommodating unique needs of migrant children in policies, programs, procedures, and school services
Standard 2: Management, Coordination, and Collaboration
    A. Shared responsibility for the instruction of migrant students attending school in more than one district or state
    B. Shared responsibility of the assessment of migrant students attending school in more than one district or state
    C. Managing data for informed decision making
Standard 3: High Expectations and Positive Attitudes
    A. Positive learning environment
    B. High expectations and access to challenging courses
    C. Heterogeneous grouping
    D. Attitude toward learning, school, and self
Standard 4: Creative, Optimal Learning Environment
    A. Quality teaching staff
    B. Use of appropriate teaching techniques and strategies
    C. Curriculum/test alignment
    D. Alternative outcome measures
Standard 5: Structures to Support Success
    A. Equitable support through health, safety, nutrition, and human services
    B. Access to home/school/community partnerships
    C. Access to staff development for all staff serving migrant students (NASDME 1994, 6–16)

Studies have also investigated successful migrant education programs (Sutton 1960; Kindler 1995; Menchaco and Ruiz-Escalente 1995; Romo 1999). These studies concur with the standards outlined by NASDME. From the studies, DiCerbo (2001) has synthesized a series of recommendations that outline effective practices "not just for individual teachers working with migrant students, but also for system-wide reform of migrant education" (DiCerbo 2001, 3). According to DiCerbo's synthesis, effective instructional programs

➼ Create a positive environment by modeling respect for diversity, and sharing experiences and values
➼ Build on migrant students' strengths by incorporating students' culture and language into the curriculum
➼ Enhance self-concept and self-esteem by giving students opportunities to demonstrate initiative, competence, and responsibility
➼ Use cooperative learning strategies to reduce anxiety and boost achievement
➼ Develop students' metacognitive learning strategies to help them become independent learners
➼ Use adequate assessment and consultation for placement decisions
➼ Implement appropriate assessment of language proficiency and academic needs
➼ Develop school leadership that makes immigrant and migrant students a priority
➼ Conduct outreach and communication in the parents' home language
➼ Provide staff development to help teachers and other staff serve immigrant students more effectively
➼ Schedule immigrant students in classes with English-speaking students (DiCerbo 2001, 3, 4)

This chapter will describe several migrant education programs that meet DiCerbo's recommendations and the standards set by NASDME. How well schools and other agencies meet DiCerbo's recommendations and the equity standards depends to a large extent on their understanding of the unique needs of the children and families they serve. Schools and other agencies that design effective programs for the migrant families and children they serve conduct needs assessments that identify the particular educational needs of the students who will be or are in their programs. Programs were selected for inclusion in this chapter based on their attention to meeting the particular needs of migrant families and children and their use of innovative practices to do so.

Summer migrant programs offer many migrant children, youth, and their families the opportunity to fill some of the academic gaps that have resulted from their mobility. The summer programs described below meet the needs of these children through a variety of formats and instructional strategies.

THE LEIPSIC, OHIO, SUMMER MIGRANT
EDUCATION PROGRAM

The Leipsic, Ohio, Local School District is in the northwest part of Ohio, a sparsely populated rural area; but the area's population grows in the summer when migrant farmworkers arrive to work in the fields. The Leipsic School District offers a summer migrant program that is administered by the Putnam County Educational Service Center.

In the summer of 2000, the summer migrant program began using the Helping One Student to Succeed (HOSTS) program to enhance literacy instruction for its first-, second-, and third-grade students. A needs assessment had shown that these young children would benefit from a structured intervention aimed at improving their English and their literacy skills.

The HOSTS program is a structured mentoring program. A commercially produced, intensive learning system, HOSTS is a nationally validated model for Title I programs and school improvement. Although the local migrant program had not previously used HOSTS, the Leipsic School District had been using HOSTS throughout the 1999–2000 school year as part of the OHIO READS initiative.

The HOSTS program, a research-based and research-validated program, is characterized by high expectations, according to Mike Walls, former school superintendent who works with schools to implement the program. Mentors in the program are trained to communicate their expectations to students that they can and will be successful. Further, HOSTS is a targeted, structured community intervention. The program is narrowly targeted toward meeting the specific learning needs of each participating student as identified by an informal reading inventory. The structure of HOSTS is designed to allow volunteer mentors from the community to work productively with students in daily one-to-one lessons that are planned individually for each student.

Volunteer mentors provide the daily one-on-one thirty-minute lessons to students. Each mentor works with a student once a week; five mentors work with each student every week. In the Leipsic summer migrant program, senior citizens, teachers, and older migrant students served as mentors. Teachers were able to participate in the program as mentors because all the students received tutoring and all the tutoring sessions with mentors were held at the same time. The HOSTS program provides mentor handbooks and formats for instructing adults and students in mentoring techniques. Mentors for the program at Leipsic received a structured orientation before they worked with students; throughout the program, the HOSTS coordinator at the school provided support and additional training informally to mentors as they worked with students.

As part of the support for HOSTS, the program inventories the instructional materials in participating schools and provides the schools with electronic databases of the instructional materials; these databases are correlated with the school's curriculum and state learning standards. Information from each student's informal reading inventory is entered into the database; the computer then generates a list of instructional materials for each of a set of learning objectives identified for that particular student. A HOSTS coordinator at the school develops a weekly lesson plan for each student that includes activities designed to develop vocabulary and reading skills, and high-quality children's literature at both the student's independent and instructional reading levels. To make sure that the lessons support the material students are studying in their classrooms, the classroom teacher may include vocabulary or instructional materials in the lesson plans.

In Leipsic, the mentor coordinator monitored the students' progress and the appropriateness of the instructional materials during the tutoring sessions. The mentor coordinator also coached mentors as they worked with the students. At the end of each tutoring session, the mentor made a record of the activities used with the student during the mentoring session and made notes about the student's progress; the next day's tutor would then have information about where to begin that day's session.

In the Leipsic summer migrant program, mentors worked with first-, second-, and third-grade students on individual lesson plans; these included high-quality children's literature that was read to them and by them, and targeted instruction in vocabulary, word identification, and identification of vowel sounds. The lesson plans dealt with specific needs identified through the informal reading inventory administered to each student at the beginning of the program. An individual set of lesson plans was developed for the tutors to use with each student.

Although the migrant students were in the program for only thirty days or less, Leipsic school personnel gathered both quantitative and anecdotal data about the students' progress in the program. Only about half the students who began the program were still in the area when the post-test was administered; the anecdotal data were gathered in anticipation of such mobility. According to information issued about the program by the Putnam County Educational Service Center, outcomes of the project were generally positive. Data from the pre- and post-testing showed significantly higher gains with the second grade students in comparison to the first grade students. Five of the seven second grade students increased their vocabulary recognition skills by one or more grade levels after HOSTS intervention. Three of the five students increased by two grade levels. All second grade students increased their vocabulary recognition skills. One of the first grade students exhibited an increase of two grade levels. Three other first grade students increased their vocabulary recognition skills. One first grade student recognized one less word when post-tested. The third grade student increased his vocabulary recognition score by eight words. (Putnam County 2000, 1)

The anecdotal data gathered included information about student responses to reading and to school in general. One child, Victor, was a nine-year-old at the time of the program. At the beginning of the summer program, Victor

did not know much of the alphabet or letter sounds. His participation in HOSTS consisted of working on the alphabet and diction. After the HOSTS intervention, he was still at the pre-primer level for vocabulary recognition, but he knew eight more words. Victor knew enough letters [and words] to read a simple book. For the first time, he began participating in class. According to his teacher, he became less disruptive and developed a helpful attitude. (Putnam County 2000, 2)

Classroom teachers reported that the students looked forward to working with their mentors, that the children had learned to enjoy reading, and that most of them had increased their socialization skills. But the children tutored were not the only ones who benefited from participating in the program. The mentors reported that they enjoyed learning from the experience as well. One of the older students in the summer program who served as a mentor to the younger children said, "This program helps me with my English while I help someone" (Putnam County 2000, 2). Based on the positive results of using HOSTS with these young children, the Leipsic summer migrant program will extend its use of HOSTS through the fourth grade in the summer of 2001.

Although the focus of the Leipsic summer migrant education program is literacy, other learning experiences are also included. Math, science, and art are taught by staff from two local universities, the University of Toledo and the University of Findlay. Students may use computers at the local public library, and the Putnam County Educational Service Center provides instruction in drug and alcohol awareness. The Leipsic summer migrant education program also offers opportunities for older students to work toward earning GEDs or preparing for the Texas Assessment of Academic Skills (TAAS) (Sealts 2000, 1).

This program meets the standard and recommendations for creating a positive learning environment and using teaching techniques that are appropriate for each learner. The documented outcomes of the program include enhanced self-esteem and self-concept for the young migrant students tutored and the older migrant students who provided the tutoring. The HOSTS program uses individual assessment and careful alignment of instruction with the assessment results. Use of tutors from the community helps to connect the migrant students to the larger community, and the use of the library computers connects the students to resources in the community outside the school. Linking with the area university for instruction in mathematics, science, and art has the potential to provide migrant children and youth with opportunities to engage in a challenging, enriched curriculum that can provide a context for learning the more basic skills and strategies.

THE KUSKO EXPRESS

The Lower Kuskokwim School District, centered in Bethel, Alaska, is 399 air miles from Anchorage. It is one of the largest rural school districts in Alaska, covering an area of about 44,000 square miles (approximately the size of Ohio). There are no roads to Bethel or to the twenty-one villages that make up the Lower Kuskokwim School District because they are situated on tundra, land that is more water than earth. In the winter, when the water and ground are frozen, ground transportation is possible by way of "snow machines." In the summer, when the water and ground are not frozen, travel around the area must be done by boat or hovercraft. Because it is dangerous to walk on the tundra during summer, boardwalks form walkways that keep feet dry, even in Bethel. The Bethel Chamber of Commerce brochure boasts sixteen miles of gravel roads within the city limits and forty-eight miles of "ice road" in the winter on the Kuskokwim River. Currently, hovercraft are being used experimentally to provide an additional means of transportation across the tundra, although there is concern about the environmental damage they may cause. The most efficient method of travel between Bethel and the villages that make up the school district, the most distant from Bethel being 120 air miles, is by plane.

The delta of the Kuskokwim River is home to moose, caribou, black bear, brown bear, musk ox, and various small game animals and birds. The Yukon Kuskokwim Delta National Wildlife Refuge, created in 1980, is the second largest national wildlife refuge in the United States.

A majority of the students in the schools in Bethel and in the villages that make up the Lower Kuskokwim School District are Yup'ik, a native Alaskan tribe. Like many other native peoples in the United States, the Yup'ik tribe is working to reestablish its native language and culture. Only a few people are fluent and literate in Yup'ik, and there is the need to tap into the knowledge of those few before the language is completely lost. The school teaches Yup'ik as a Second Language (YSL), and teachers and other community members are working to write books and other curriculum materials in English and Yup'ik about traditional Yup'ik culture. They have also translated various classic children's stories into Yup'ik to promote literacy in both languages. The bilingual department of the school district has published many books, big books, CD ROMs, books on tape, and posters in Yup'ik and Cup'ig, a dialect of Yup'ik.

During the summer months, members of the Yup'ik tribe migrate from Bethel and the other villages to subsistence fishing camps on the shores of the Kuskokwim River and its branches. Families camp there during the season to catch and preserve fish for their own use. Students are eligible for the migrant education program because of these moves. In the fishing camps, families have radio and VHS, but no television. There are only four hours of darkness in the summer, so days are long, and there are few diversions for the children.

Providing a summer migrant education program and keeping the students from the Lower Kuskokwim School District reading over the summer months when they were at the fishing camps presented a challenge. It is impossible for the school district to conduct a summer school program that brings children together in school buildings, and fishing camps are remote and have no facilities for summer school programs.

Educators in the Lower Kuskokwim School District created an innovative program that takes books to the children via the Kusko Book Express. In the summer of 2000, about 1,200 students participated in the third year of the Kusko Book Express; books were taken to them at the fishing camps, in the villages, and in Bethel. Combining migrant education program funds with other school district funds and funding from a variety of community sources, the program uses boats, a bookmobile, and school district personnel and workers in nine villages to deliver reading and writing materials to children and youth from the school district.

To recruit students and families at the fishing camps to participate in the Kusko Book Express, school district educators traveled by boat to the fishing camps along the Kuskokwim River and the side rivers to talk with parents and children, ages three through nineteen, about the program. After that, crews from the school district traveled the more than eighty miles of rivers on two boats, delivering books and journals once each week, discussing books that children have read and the writing they have done in their journals, reading aloud and telling stories to children, and awarding prizes for reading books and writing about them. The crew members encouraged parents to read with their children, to talk with their children about the books they read, and to model reading for them. The Kusko Book Express provides local newspapers to parents so that they have reading material themselves. With these reading materials, parents can model reading for their children.

One member of the crew that delivers books is the principal of a village elementary school. When he visits the fishing camps, he sings with the children and tells stories using a traditional Yup'ik story knife. In the Yup'ik culture, storytelling is accompanied by drawing symbols in the sand with a story knife; these symbols represent events from the stories. Elsie Waite, a Lower Kuskokwim School District teacher and Kusko Book Express crew member, noted that the "story knife tradition" is one that is also disappearing; Yup'ik educators are working to restore this tradition.

Lenora Arnold, the Kusko Book Express program coordinator, reported that children eager to tell the crew members about the books they've read and to select new books, often meet the boats as they arrive at the fishing camps. Children look forward to choosing from the selections of books provided for their grade levels. The collections of books, some of which are in English and some in Yup'ik, include books the children will be expected to read during the next school year. When children read the books during the summer, they gain a head start on their school work when they begin school in the fall. Children are encouraged to select as many books as they can read; the program coordinator reports trying to supply specific books children ask for.

In Bethel, a bookmobile travels around town, delivering books and journals to children there each week. Some children also stay in the villages during the summer. Books are delivered by plane to children in eight nearby villages, and workers in the villages distribute the books. Many of the workers distribute the books from their homes; some of them set regular times each week for distribution, and others make books available as children are ready for them.

In the third year of the program, summer 2000, readers read from one to fifteen books. Lenora Arnold reports encouraging families to keep the books to start family libraries or add to them. The school district newsletter, *Elicaq* (Yup'ik for "teaching and learning"), summed up a story about the program: "Children are reading, parents are reading and the connection between parents and LKSD is being strengthened" (Arnold 2000, 10).

The Kusko Book Express meets several of the standards and recommendations for migrant education programs. The program is sensitive to and meets the unique and specific needs, context, and culture of the migrant children and youth it serves. It has also addressed students' attitudes toward themselves and reading; students in the program have come to enjoy reading and look forward to their journaling and book discussions. The program focuses on home-school partnerships and building intergenerational literacy through the provision of reading materials to parents. The program incorporates the students' culture and language through the reading materials it provides in Yup'ik and honors such cultural traditions as using the story knife. Children have opportunities to learn metacognitive skills through journaling about and discussing the books that they read.

BEST S.E.L.F.

In two counties in Washington state, the Migrant Education Program works in collaboration with the county governments and school districts, as well as a number of other funding sources, in what could be called value-added summer and school year extended-day programs. This program is called Best S.E.L.F. (Summer Education and Learning Fun).

Best S.E.L.F. began in Skagit County in 1992, its mission being to provide "an enriching summer experience for children, serve families, and to foster community involvement and collaboration" (Best S.E.L.F. 2001, 1). From its first summer of serving 230 children in two schools, the program has grown to seven school districts. Best S.E.L.F., which has grown in Skagit County in collaboration with seventeen active agency and business partners, now serves over 1,600 children. In 2001, the Best S.E.L.F. program in Skagit County was awarded a 21st Century grant. This grant allows the program to include a school year extended-day program for elementary students, as well as a half-day program for kindergarten that extends the state-funded half-day program to a full day. In 1997, the Migrant Education Program became a partner in this collaborative effort; in 1999, the program was replicated in Yakima County, which anticipated serving children in eight schools in six school districts in 2001. Two four-week sessions are provided each summer; students may enroll in the program for the full eight weeks. The summer program operates Monday through Friday from 7:30 a.m. to 5:30 p.m. The core curriculum, activities, and field trips occur between 9:00 a.m. and 3:00 p.m.; before and after those hours, extended-day services are provided to accommodate parents' schedules. Children in the program are served breakfast, lunch, and snacks. Transportation for all field trips and community service projects is provided through Best S.E.L.F. The Washington State Migrant Education Program provides transportation to and from the Best S.E.L.F. schools for migrant children.

The Best S.E.L.F. program is funded through several sources, including the county governments and local businesses, and grants. It is also partially tuition-funded; students who are eligible for the Migrant Education Program are provided scholarships from the Migrant Education Program. In the summer of 2000, nearly one-third of the children who participated in the Yakima County program were eligible for the Migrant Education Program and received the scholarships.

The Best S.E.L.F. program has three components, each of which accounts for one-third of the program: recreation, which consists of active, rich, traditional and nontraditional activities; hands-on kinesthetic and experiential learning; and service learning and community involvement. Recreation activities include hiking, rock climbing, skating, noncompetitive sports, and challenge courses. The recreation activities often involve challenges and higher-order thinking activities such as chess, math games, and scientific problems (Hansen 2001, 13).

Children engage in hands-on, kinesthetic, and experiential learning that is aligned with the Washington State Learning Standards and Essential Academic Learning Requirements. Learning experiences are thematic and designed to "inspire students to develop positive associations with learning" (Hansen 2001, 14). Students take field trips to extend their learning outside the classroom and to take advantage of resources within the community. These trips provide a rich experience base upon which to build vocabulary and concepts. In a videotape about Best S.E.L.F., students are shown on a whale-watching trip. A group of children described one whale they had seen: "We adopted a whale. Her name is Oreo. She has one baby." "You can tell it's her because she has a jagged thing on her back. So whenever you go whale-watching, you can watch for Oreo" (Best S.E.L.F. 1999).

Children also participate in service learning, such as mural painting, that allow them to participate as citizens of their communities. Such activities are designed to help children feel connected to one another and the community, to encourage a sense of pride in themselves and the community, and to extend academic learning outside of the classroom. One group of kindergarten children, for example, painted a mural on a fence at a senior citizens' center. The senior citizens who worked with the children to design the mural requested that the mural include mountains. The children's painting provided a source of entertainment for the senior citizens as they watched the the mural being painted. While they worked on the mural, the children had lunch with the senior citizens; when the mural was completed, the senior citizens' center provided swimming lessons for the children. In another service learning project, students worked to create a gravel path at a nature center. One of the students remarked to a teacher, "You know, after putting all this gravel down and building this trail, I really have respect for outdoors and Parks and Rec'. I will never kick gravel off this trail again" (Best S.E.L.F. 1999).

Judy Jacobson, program director for Yakima County Best S.E.L.F., reported that cutbacks at the Parks Department had resulted in a lack of funds to maintain a rose garden in the community. Students in the Best S.E.L.F. program worked at the rose garden, doing the necessary clean up and pruning in exchange for a day of swimming.

A fourth component is especially important for the migrant children who participate in the program. This component is a link between social service agencies and the program "to identify and recruit students with special needs" (Hansen 1999, 15).

Children who might be isolated from the larger community, such as children of mobile farmworker families, experience a feeling of belonging when working in teams on service learning projects. The intent is to

- Identify children who can benefit
- Encourage agencies and schools to refer and support these children
- Bring special populations into unique community relationships
- Allow the large community to experience and enjoy the beauty and creativity of a diverse segment of the population (Hansen 1999, 15)

Migrant children are fully integrated with the community children in the Best S.E.L.F. program. They sit together, they learn together, and they work on teams together in community service projects.

Best S.E.L.F. has formed a relationship with Washington State University to develop an assessment for the program. In the meantime, Best S.E.L.F. has received several awards and recognitions for its quality. In 1999, Best S.E.L.F. received the multicultural and diversity award of the National Association of County Organizations, as well as an award for its potential as a model program by the Johnson Foundation. Best S.E.L.F. also received a Golden Tennis Shoe award from Washington state senator Patty Murray.

Most important, though, are the positive results of the program. Skagit County program director Tawni Helms explained that the Best

S.E.L.F. program has been received positively by parents, program personnel, the children in the program, and the larger community. According to Mike Woodmansee, the administrator for Skagit County, "We fill kids' minds. We fill their stomachs. We fill their summers with activity and enrichment. . . . They go back to school better citizens. They go back to school better learners. They go back to school feeling better about themselves and ready to tackle the demands that school and the opportunity to succeed puts on all of us" (Best S.E.L.F. 1999).

For migrant students, the Best S.E.L.F. program is "value-added"; the collaboration of the Migrant Education Program with county government, school districts involved, and business and community resources results in a program that greatly extends what the Migrant Education Program could provide by itself. Washington State Migrant Education Program personnel cite the following reasons for their collaboration with Best S.E.L.F.:

- Migrant students are included in all activities: academic, service, and enrichment.
- Migrant students are connected to the community through service-based projects.
- Migrant students are offered up to fifty hours of enrichment per week.
- Bilingual and multicultural staff are recruited and hired to encourage cultural sensitivity for all (Best S.E.L.F. 2001, 2)

A classroom teacher in Yakima County noted that an additional benefit for migrant students is that they are entering school in the fall feeling connected with the school and with a peer group of students.

Children in the Best S.E.L.F. program are served by a staff that includes certified teachers, college and university students, and high school students, resulting in a ratio of one staff member to five children in each classroom. A maximum of thirty students are enrolled in each classroom. An At Risk Intervention Specialist (A.R.I.S.) team is available at each site to provide immediate support to classroom teaching teams, ensuring that all students have educational experiences that are appropriate and that meet their particular learning needs.

A further benefit to the Migrant Education Program and migrant students is that the Skagit County program regularly employs high school migrant students during the day in the summer. These students then participate in evening sessions to work on their Portable Assisted Study Sequence (PASS) courses.

Best S.E.L.F. has expanded beyond the summer program to provide extended day programs at elementary schools in their partner school districts. These after-school programs have the same recreation, education, and service learning components as the summer programs. Best S.E.L.F. has also begun supplementing the half-day kindergarten programs funded by the state with additional half-day programs for kindergarten children.

The Best S.E.L.F. program provides a high-quality educational experience for migrant children. It also helps them to feel that they belong in the school, and that they are part of a community in which they can take pride and that takes pride in them.

The partnership between the Washington State Migrant Education Program and the Best S.E.L.F. program meets the NASDME standard for equitable resources and financing; the combination of community funding and support with migrant program funds provide access for migrant students to high-quality educational programming that includes the use of technology, developmentally appropriate instruction, and a challenging curriculum. At the same time, a support team is available to help classroom teachers meet the unique needs of these children. The Best S.E.L.F. program has a positive learning environment that communicates high expectations for all the students in the program, and migrant students work together with nonmigrant students. The experiential and hands-on learning in the Best S.E.L.F. program is aligned with the state of Washington learning standards, and the support services that migrant children need—health, nutrition, safety, and social services—are available to them through the program.

Best S.E.L.F. also typifies DiCerbo's recommendations for migrant education. The program is built around honoring diversity, and students have opportunities to learn about each other first hand as they work together on learning teams and on community service teams. The A.R.I.S. team provides assessments of students' needs as well as consultations with teachers to ensure that students' learning needs are being met. This is a program that meets the intent of both the standards for equity for migrant students and the recommendations for effective instructional programs.

HARVEST OF HOPE

In 2000, the Pennsylvania Migrant Education Program began a collaboration with the Youtheater, the youth company affiliated with the Fulton Opera House. The Fulton Opera House, in Lancaster, Pennsylvania, is the oldest operating theater in the United States. The collaboration led to a unique summer program for a group of twelve high school migrant students. These migrant students worked with other young performers to write, produce, and perform in a play about the migrant experience during the six-week education experience at the theater.

Students at the Pennsylvania Migrant Education Student Leadership Institute wrote about their experiences, and those of their extended families, as migrants. The twelve migrant students who were involved in the theater project developed a play from those writings. At the same time, the students were working to learn about the theater and about acting, singing, and dancing on stage.

The original production, *Harvest of Hope*, included original music, lyrics, dance, and dialogue to explain to an audience what it means to teenagers to be migrant. "The student actor-singer-dancers express how it felt always to be moving, never knowing where they would end up, how it felt to arrive late in a new school and not comprehending the teacher because of a language barrier. They reveal the typical teenage anxieties and uncertainties, while trying to maintain the strength and courage to survive in the face of prejudice, low expectations and economic hardships" (*Harvest of Hope* 2001, 10).

One scene in the play, for example, portrayed the experience of a migrant student's going to a new school and not understanding English. The teacher, whose English sounded like "blah, blah, blah, blah, blah" to the non-English-speaking student, communicated frustration with, and contempt for, the student, while the student tried desperately to follow what he thought the teacher was directing him to do.

Another recurring theme in the play was leaving. In several scenarios in the play, as students developed relationships with one another, they abruptly announced that they were moving. Hiding from and evading immigration officials were also portrayed.

The migrant students performed the play with five students who were deaf and one who was legally blind. These actors were intentionally reverse typecast, members of the cast taking on the life roles of other cast members. "This device makes each student's struggle a struggle for all students as they spur each other forward in building positive outlooks on their future" (*Harvest of Hope* 2001, 10).

The play was performed in a three-week run at the Fulton Opera House and in a special performance in the opening session of the 2001 National Migrant Education Conference in Orlando, Florida.

The *Harvest of Hope* project was an innovative one that met many of the equity standards and the recommendations for migrant education programs. The project offered a challenging curriculum that included writing and constructing history, stagecraft, and acting. Migrant students worked together with nonmigrant students, some of whom were also hearing and vision impaired, in the project; together they engaged in a project that focused on understanding the diverse life experiences and life histories of the students in the theater program. Migrant students in the project had opportunities to take initiative and to work creatively, building positive self-concept and self-esteem in the process.

THE UNIVERSITY OF TEXAS AT AUSTIN MIGRANT STUDENT GRADUATION ENHANCEMENT PROGRAM

The University of Texas at Austin (UT Austin) Migrant Student Graduation Enhancement Program began in 1987 as an effort to assist Texas middle school and high school students to take Texas high school courses wherever they went, even out of state. This program is administered through the University Distance Education Center and funded through the Texas Migrant Education Program and a Graduation Enhancement Grant.

The UT Austin program offers students the opportunity to take courses that are required for graduation from Texas high schools either for credit at their own middle or high schools in Texas or on a transcript issued by the university. All the courses offered are approved by the Texas Education Agency and fulfill the Texas Essential Knowledge and Skills requirements. Students may register and begin courses at any time; once registered, students have nine months to complete a course.

Courses are offered in a variety of formats designed to meet the needs of students. First, the program offers Credit by Examination. In the Credit by Examination option, students can take an exam to earn credit for courses in English, mathematics, social studies, health, and Spanish. When students register for a Credit by Examination course, UT Austin provides them with review sheets they can use to prepare for the exams. The exams are written by "certified teachers with subject-matter expertise" (Sutton 2000a, 33). The tests may be proctored either by a UT instructor or a migrant educator in Texas or another state. The tests are then scored by UT instructors. For each course, two different tests are offered. Students who have had no instruction in the subject take the Examination for Acceleration; they earn credit if they score 90 percent or better. Students who have had instruction take the Credit by Examination test; they earn credit if they score at least 70 percent.

The UT Austin Migrant Student Graduation Enhancement Program also offers courses for credit by correspondence. Each of the courses earns one-half credit. The courses are designed to "optimize student learning" by including the following:

- Short study units and vocabulary review to ensure comprehension of content and to improve language and vocabulary skills
- Commentary that explains and demonstrates subject matter in clear, concise language
- Appropriate, effective visual presentations that reinforce course elements
- Various objective activities that give students ample opportunities to apply and practice new knowledge and skills
- Writing exercises that invite students to relate subject matter to their own lives (Sutton 2000a, 31)

Students receive study guides that include the nine to twelve lessons developed for each course and textbooks from the program.

When students take one of the twenty-two courses offered as correspondence courses, they work through the lessons on their own and return them to the university for feedback and grades from a university instructor. In this case, when they have completed the coursework, students must take the final exam either at UT Austin or at a site approved by the university.

Migrant students also have the option of taking the courses in receiving schools, where Migrant Education Program teachers work with the students to complete the lessons, give immediate feedback, and administer the final exams. When students work on the courses in Migrant Education Program classrooms, UT Austin provides answer keys to the teachers. Migrant Education Program teachers may also administer the final exams; the exams are sent to UT Austin for scoring.

The UT Austin Migrant Student Graduation Enhancement Program offers some courses electronically. One course, Algebra Across the Wire, is an audio interactive distance learning format for Algebra I. This teleconferenced course has a teacher at one site and small groups of students at other sites. Teleconferencing technology allows for the course to be interactive, with real time communication, both video and audio, that connects the teacher to each of the sites and all the sites to each other. The class meets on a regular schedule. It has the highest completion rate of any of these courses—90 percent (Sutton 2000a, 31)—due at least in part to the direct teacher-student interaction, and because students have to verbalize mathematics concepts and operations as they interact with their teachers and other students.

Two for-credit courses are offered as courses on disk, Government on a Disk, and Health on a Disk, both required for graduation in Texas. These courses, on CD ROM, which consist of a series of lessons similar to those in the correspondence courses, are interactive and provide immediate feedback to students. Also available on disk are two courses that are not for credit—mathematics preparation for the exit level TAAS and Marketing Yourself.

One online course is available: Mathematical Models with Applications, first semester. UT Austin provides a laptop computer for each migrant student who registers for this course, connection to the Internet, a graphing calculator, and training for using the Internet. This online course is interactive, and it takes advantage of the Internet to offer such capabilities as a weekly chat room, audio conferencing, e-mail, and communication with a distant teacher. The course material is divided into units, each with its own menu. It includes application and practice problems, a "unit problem," which allows students to put all the skills and concepts learned in the unit together, and a "your turn" section, in which students are asked to use the new learning to create a problem of their own. Assessments are also provided online. The distant instructor grades students' work and gives feedback.

Although the electronic course offerings are small, a grant from Microsoft will support the development of more courses on disk, as well as more online courses. UT Austin expects to have more complete courses, or at least a component of nearly every course, available on disk within the near future.

One additional option for migrant students is to take courses for partial credit. Students who have already completed part of a course at a school may complete that course through the UT Austin program.

Texas counselors are available to help students make decisions about which courses to take. Counselors are also available to work with migrant educators who work with Texas students on these courses in receiving schools in other states. The university provides follow-up support to migrant students in the program as well.

The UT Austin Migrant Student Program involves parents in the distance learning courses. The program provides print and face-to-face information to parents; it also expects parents to sign contracts along with their children for completing the work.

The UT Austin Migrant Student Program helps nearly 1,000 students every year complete courses and earn credit toward graduation. Every year, many of the students graduate from high school, and some of them even complete their high school programs in three years, in spite of all the barriers they face. UT Austin honors some of the students at the end of the year for their outstanding work. The majority of the exemplary migrant students recognized in 2000, according to the UT Austin Migrant Student Program, "have migrated frequently, leaving their Texas schools early in the spring and returning late in the fall every school year, thus making their education a challenge. The [students recognized in 2000] attend[ed] seventeen different Texas schools and have migrated with their families to nineteen different states, as far away as New York and Washington" (Sutton 2000a, 1). The students recognized were all planning to go to college, breaking the cycle of migrant labor and poverty in which they grew up.

The UT Austin Migrant Student Program meets several of the equity standards and the recommendations for migrant education programs. First, the program offers access to resources that extend the instructional programs the students have in school programs. It meets the standard for shared responsibility for both instruction and assessment, as well as for management of data. The project provides the students with access to challenging courses and opportunities to keep up with their nonmigrating peers in course accrual and graduation. Courses are aligned with the TAAS, meeting the standard for alignment between curriculum and testing.

The UT Austin Migrant Student Graduation Enhancement Program meets the recommendations for building self-esteem and self-concept through the opportunity for independent learning. Students are placed in courses based on assessment; the program includes outreach and communication with parents. And, most important, the program provides migrant students with the opportunity to prepare for postsecondary education, as many of the students do each year.

Several current migrant education projects use technology, as well as other research-based strategies, to address several of the factors that interfere with educational success for migrant students. Distance learning has the potential to help students maintain communication with their home schools and and to break down the social isolation that is such a factor in migrant education. The UT Austin Migrant Student Graduation Enhancement Program is beginning to take advantage of distance learning technologies. ★Estrella is a project that demonstrates just how effective distance technology can be in breaking down the barriers that the migrant lifestyle puts in the way of migrant students' educational success.

★ESTRELLA

Administered by the Illinois Migrant Council and funded by the U.S. Department of Education Office of Migrant Education, ★Estrella is a five-year interstate project whose goal is "to demonstrate the applicability of technology to the education and advancement of migrant farmworker students" (★Estrella 2001a). The project works at twenty-one sites in five states to help students complete their high school educations and graduate, and to create in the students a vision for participating in postsecondary education.

Potential students are identified for the program first through information in the New Generation System (NGS); they must have a home base in one of six school districts in Texas and migrate to Illinois, Minnesota, Montana, and New York. The six Texas school districts in the project are Eagle Pass, La Joya, Mercedes, Pharr-San Juan-Alamo, San Felipe-Del Rio, and Weslaco.

From the pool of identified students, participants are selected based on the recommendations of local migrant project directors, high school teachers, and Texas home-base school personnel, and a series of criteria that include interest, need for credit accrual, a high level of parental support, academic success and motivation, telephone access, computer literacy, and study skills. High school juniors and seniors are given first priority for participation in the program (★Estrella 2001b).

Each student who participates in ★Estrella receives a laptop computer. The laptop computer allows access to NovaNET, an online curriculum and instructional delivery system that offers courses at both the middle school and high school level that students can use for course and credit completion. Students also receive Internet accounts; these give students and their families access to the resources available online. Information from the students' home-base school is used to determine the courses that students take online; teachers in the receiving schools provide instruction in addition to online offerings as needed by the students. According to the ★Estrella project description, "Teachers keep track of their students' course work progress by using the record keeping information maintained by NovaNET. A complete history of each students' work can be viewed at any time. . . . NovaNET stores the students' most recent tests, which allows instructors to view any errors and review the test with the student. Upon satisfactory completion of course work, students receive credit issued by their Texas home-base school district" (★Estrella, 2001d).

Many of the students involved in ★Estrella work in the fields during the day, and work on their academic coursework in the evening. Deysi, a student from Eagle Pass ISD, in Eagle Pass, Texas, who participated in the summer migrant program in Sidney, Montana, wrote about her summer schedule:

The Long, Long Summer
This was a very long summer of 2000. I came to Sidney, Montana, with my family like I do every year to work in the sugar beets for a month. This was the first year I planned to go to night school because I wanted to complete a course for credit to help me graduate from high school. The lessons were hard but it was worth the headache to get a half credit without having to go to school for a whole semester. That's good because that will help me graduate. Everyday after working on the laptop, my teacher, Arlene Hueth, who is real fun and understanding, gave us time to relax for a few minutes before the bus picked us up to drive us home. David and Lori Camarillo, from Texas, were teachers who spent the summer in Montana to help in the migrant program. They were a lot of fun.

When I first got to Sidney, Arlene told me about a program that was paying students for going to school after the long hard labor work days. Mike Rea was our sponsor for the Youth Program that was compensating us for coming to school. This program was helpful because it encouraged students to come to school no matter how tired they were. (★Estrella 2000, 6)

An additional instructional component in ★Estrella is that of visual learning. To support student communication in general, and writing in particular, the project combines technology with visual learning methods. Students are encouraged to use instant imaging and scanning technology to enhance their work, and participating teachers are provided with a copy of *Visual Learning Teacher's Guide,* a handbook developed by project staff to assist teachers in using instant cameras, scanners, and computers to motivate students to write.

Amanda, an ★Estrella student from San Felipe-Del Rio ISD, in Del Rio, Texas, participated in the summer migrant program in Princeville, Illinois, in the summer of 2000. She reflected on her visual learning project:

When I started on this protect, I wanted to capture the sheer struggle of the elderly working as migrants. I didn't have time to take pictures. You see, I work at a canning company. At times I work up to fourteen hours straight and then have to go to school. So I ended up taking these that you see. As I look at them I realize that I captured my friends' and my daily fight: long hours at work versus making the grade. I sometimes wake up and find myself at school, not knowing how or when I got

there. Sooner or later my grades are hurting as is my body for it yearns
for rest. Many times my mind is numb as if my body is put in pilot and
doing everything automatically. Is this a small price to pay
for the dead presidents I see every Friday? Mr. Lincoln on the one
dollar bill, Mr. Jackson on the twenty. Is it all for the money? (★Estrella
2000, 10)

Each student in the ★Estrella project is assigned a cyber mentor
from the University of Texas Pan American in Edinburg, Texas. These
cyber mentors, who are participants in the College Assistance Migrant
Program (CAMP) program at the University of Texas Pan American, regularly communicate by e-mail with their mentees. The mentors, who are
from migrant families themselves, bring understanding of and empathy
with Hispanic and migrant culture. The mentors can all say, "If I can do
it, you can, too!" As such, they are positive role models for ★Estrella students. Further, they provide information about career options and support for the transition to postsecondary education, including assistance
with applying for admission, scholarships, and financial aid. They also
provide a social connection, so important to students who are often socially isolated because of their frequent mobility. According to ★Estrella's
program description, the mentors also "share their experiences in decid-
ing to pursue postsecondary education, choosing a school and field of
study, living on or off campus, and balancing study and work commit-
ments" (★Estrella 2001c). Mentors and mentees meet annually in person
at a university campus. This activity provides the opportunity for mentors and mentees to get to know each other better; it also provides
mentees with an experience on a university campus.

    ★Estrella works to provide other experiences that create a vision
for postsecondary education for its participants as well as an understanding of a variety of career options. Michelle, an ★Estrella student
from Mercedes, Texas, participated in the summer migrant program in
Kankakee, Illinois, during the summers of 1999 and 2000. As part of that
program, she had the opportunity to visit Northern Illinois University
(NIU). She wrote about that experience in *Estupendas Laptop Talk,* the
newsletter published by ★Estrella. She began by recalling her experience in 1999:

I am in high school and can't imagine what college life is all about. I
thought of being lost out there and afraid of what to expect. That was
what I thought last year before going to NIU.

    This year I knew what to expect, but I knew that some way or an-
other it would be different. I was told that there would be a different

group of students there and I didn't know what to expect from this different group. I didn't know whether I would get along with them or not. . . .

Last year on campus there was a group of kids that were deaf. I wanted to learn how to communicate with them. . . . This year my friend taught me sign language just in case the deaf students came back so I could communicate with them or maybe they could teach me more. So I was hoping they would be back! My mind on the bus didn't know what to expect.

During the day, the students would go to different job sites and see what workers did. I would stay behind and work on my U.S. government course in the mornings. In the afternoons I got to go with the students and I went to a factory where they made seats for Neon Chrysler cars and to the fire station. Those two jobs, I am not saying they are bad, but it is not what I want to do when I grow up. I don't want to work at the factory because I am the type of person that gets bored doing the same things over and over throughout the day and I wouldn't like that job. Being a firefighter is not for me because I don't like ambulances and tragedies; I would probably get nervous at the last minute and put somebody's life in danger. I want to go to college and study for something that I am good at and will like to do for the rest of my life. I want to wake up every day anxious and excited to get to my job.

I did get to meet the deaf students, after all. I learned how to sign a bit, to communicate and understand what they tried to tell me. I understood that being deaf means they can't talk on the phone or listen to music like a regular teen. It makes me think of how lucky I am to be able to do those things. I never took those things into consideration before. These are the things I learned about their way of life. This was one of the high points of the week at NIU for me. (★Estrella 2000, 2)

Parental involvement is an important component of ★Estrella. In addition to signing a contract with the program to protect and maintain the computer hardware provided by the program, parents also agree to "provide an atmosphere that encourages their children's participation in the program" (★Estrella 2001e). In return, parents and family members receive computer training themselves, allowing them the opportunity to access such NovaNET resources as GED materials and preparation, courses for learning English and other adult basic education, and citizenship information. ★Estrella also provides parents with information about access to postsecondary education, including "how to seek information about college, how to pay for college and how to apply for admission and financial aid (★Estrella 2001e). Parents are invited with their children to attend workshops on university campuses, so that they also learn about the culture of the university along with their children.

An additional ★Estrella component is that of professional development for teachers and other personnel who serve the migrant students who are participants in the project. The intent of this professional development is to provide a vehicle through which teachers can collaborate between schools and states in support of student learning and to assist teachers in facilitating classroom learning experiences and projects that complement, extend, and enhance the NovaNET curriculum. Although much of the professional development is provided online, ★Estrella also brings all the teachers together at one site at least once a year so that they can work together face-to-face and establish relationships that support their collaborative involvement with the students. Students are also invited to participate in the professional development activities of the project to make them active agents in the development of their own learning activities. To facilitate this collaboration of students and teachers, ★Estrella has a Working Web Home Page that provides a forum for them to participate together in professional development. To validate the work of ★Estrella participants and to provide an opportunity for students and teachers to publish their work, the project publishes an online newsletter, *Estupendas Laptop Talk.*

The project director of ★Estrella, Brenda Pessin of the Illinois Migrant Council, reported that in the fourth year, seventeen participants have graduated. Of those, 47 percent are currently enrolled in college; one is in the military; and 29 percent are working and making plans to attend college. Twelve percent of the graduates are working and not planning to attend college at this time.

The first ★Estrella participant graduated from high school in February 1999, and is currently enrolled in college. She has achieved this in spite of great odds; married and a mother at age sixteen, this young woman earned her high school diploma with the support of ★Estrella and a migrant Even Start project, Tiempo de Valor. According to *Estupendas,*

> Annie has benefited from her participation in many programs. As a young child, she attended Migrant Head Start every summer until she entered kindergarten. During her grade school and high school years, she attended the Princeville Migrant Education Program. While in ★Estrella, Annie also enrolled in Tiempo de Valor, a Migrant Even Start Program in which she and her young son participated in family literacy activities.

In July 2000 Tiempo de Valor offered Annie employment as a home visitor even though she had very little experience and background. Accepting the challenge with wholehearted dedication, she has been working with parents and their children ages two to six, providing them with educational activities in their home. She also helps first and second graders with their homework and advocates for them in the local school district by informing parents of their rights and encouraging them to speak with the teachers about their children's education. Annie has accomplished her duties by taking all that has been positive in her life and giving it to the migrant families with whom she works. She is helping them to set their own personal goals and on to achieve them.

This young adult is not special because she has overcome barriers or is actively pursuing her education. Annie [is special and] will succeed largely due to her eagerness to assist the population she has always been part of. Annie has become a true role model! (★Estrella 2000, 19)

★Estrella is a project that represents all the standards and recommendations in practice. The project meets the standard for equity of access; students have access to the technology and the instructional resources they need in a form that accommodates their migrant lifestyle through the laptops provided in the program. There is shared responsibility for both instruction and assessment among students' home-base schools, the schools they attend in the summer, and the ★Estrella project. ★Estrella works to communicate high expectations and a positive learning environment; the technology and cyber mentor components contribute to an optimal learning environment that helps students to create a vision for postsecondary education. The staff development component and parent component are structures that support success for the students who participate in the project.

★Estrella also portrays DiCerbo's recommendations for effective instructional migrant education programs. Student writing in the project allows them to share experiences and values; publishing that writing in the project newsletter has the potential to contribute to building student self-esteem. Students' visual learning projects demonstrate their use of metacognitive learning strategies, as well as how those strategies have contributed to helping them learn independently. The focus on creating a vision for postsecondary education is strengthened by the involvement of parents in learning about college life, admissions, and financial aid. The strong staff development component of ★Estrella contributes to its success; including students in that staff development communicates that they truly are members of this unique community of learners.

CONEXIONES

Conexiones is another migrant education project that uses technology to meet the needs of migrant students. The Conexiones Project, in operation since 1992, has as its purpose "to encourage life-long learning and to increase both educational and occupational opportunities among traditionally underserved minority students through the use of technology" (Conexiones 2001, 1). Conexiones is a technology-based education program designed to address the unique educational needs of migrant students. At the same time, the project works to support teachers and schools who serve those students, and develop a community to support the education of migrant youth that includes the migrant students themselves, their families, their teachers, university faculty members, university students, and researchers. The project brings together resources from a large number of partner organizations. These include the Arizona Department of Migrant Education, Arizona State University College of Education, and a number of other national and local organizations and businesses, including the Arizona State Public Information Network, Apple, the Public Broadcasting System (PBS), Macromedia, Intel, and LEGO.

To address the unique educational needs of migrant students, Conexiones has created "an environment of respect and trust, challenging students with curricula designed to help them develop English language and technological fluency, and supporting students by helping them to develop a university-wide network of students, mentors, and educators" (Conexiones 2001, 1). The project also helps migrant students to be "fluent users rather than passive consumers" of technology. Students in the project are involved in designing and programming computer applications, developing skills that allow the students to connect to one another technologically, and to access scientists, engineers, and computer experts (Conexiones 2001, 2). They have opportunities to explore, learn about, and solve problems through object-oriented and HTML programming, image processing, graphics production, Web-based instruction, and programmable Legos.

Migrant students of middle and high school age in the project are involved in constructivist and project-based bilingual literacy and technology learning activities through Conexiones that lead to meeting Arizona State Standards in technology, science, mathematics, and language arts. In the summer of 1999, for example, students in the program "spent two weeks building, programming, and testing autonomous robots" as part of the Lego Engineers, Inc. program. In this program, students, working in groups of four, form a company to design a Lego robot that addresses a set of guidelines presented to them. "In addition, students also designed company Web sites to present and market their robots to the community at large." Students chose from a list of projects that included such robots as Swamp Navigator, Latinos Nuclear Waste Cleaner "2000," Speedy Wheels, Power Wheelchairs, Cranes, First class Windmills, and The Funky Forklift (Conexiones 1999, 1). The guidelines for one of the projects, the Swamp Navigator, are shown in Figure 5.1.

In addition to the robot projects, students also participated in online lessons in technology (e-mail, the Internet), stable structures (structural integrity with pennies), and science (gears). The lessons and their assessments were all cross-referenced with the Arizona Educational Standards; students developed portfolios of their work, as well as Web sites, that documented their learning in the project. Information about specific standards and student achievement related to those standards can be found at http://conexiones.asu.edu/curriculum.html.

During the summer of 2000, thirty-two students in the Conexiones Project "learned to convey information effectively, to interpret situations insightfully, and to express their ideas through the application of advanced digital video production and post-production techniques." Each student wrote, produced, directed, and edited a video production of a public service announcement. The video projects can be viewed at http://conexiones.asu.edu/summer00video/html.

Because the program is offered on the university campus, students have the opportunity to learn about higher education at the same time that they develop skills and concepts that help them to meet the Arizona State Standards. This opportunity helps to familiarize students with the culture and context of higher education, so critical to students' developing a vision for their own participation in higher education.

A further goal of the Conexiones Project is to explore and investigate "emerging learning technologies, innovative teaching strategies for both minority and technologically integrated education, and effective evaluation and assessment of student performance" (Conexiones 1999, 2). The curriculum development that is part of the Conexiones Project has resulted in the creation of model standards-based lessons and performance assessments, all disseminated through the project's Conexiones Clearinghouse. This work, in turn, helps to support classroom teachers and schools who work with migrant students on a regular basis.

The Conexiones project also recognizes the importance of parent and family involvement in students' education. Families are invited and encouraged to participate in many of the project's activities, including students' final presentations at the end of each Conexiones session.

FIGURE 5.1   Sample Project Guidelines

THE SWAMP NAVIGATOR CHALLENGE

Design Brief

Your Uncle Arturo retired last year and moved east—he actually exchanged his farmland in Phoenix for swampland in Louisiana. You thought he was a little nuts, especially when he called to ask you and your design team to build a Swamp Navigator. He's suddenly obsessed with documenting everything that lives in his swamp. At first you blew it off, thinking that his sudden interest in nature will fade just as suddenly as it began. But he's serious. In fact, he just sent your team first-class airplane tickets. In two weeks, you're supposed to fly to Florida with a model of your design. Arturo is so confident that your ideas will be brilliant that he's invited a mechanical engineer for dinner on the day you arrive. (In addition to swamp navigating, Arturo also has taken up cooking since he retired.)

Design Features

These are the things that Arturo wants in his Swamp Navigator. He's sending you those plane tickets, so don't disappoint him by leaving any of these things out! That Swamp Navigator must:

- Move forward, backward, and side-to-side
- Move over different types of terrain (sand, mud, rocks, etc.)
- Be controlled by user
- Move with legs, NOT wheels
- Move through water
- Move across all kinds of underwater

Getting Started on Design

Go to the Conexiones Web site. Look at what other people have created. Soon you'll get a sense of the great potential of Lego Robotics. But other people's ideas aren't going to match all of Arturo's requirements. So this is only a place to start.

http://conexiones.asu.edu/curriculum/roboticideas.html

Think About the Client

Arturo's gotten a little crazy since he retired. He'll be really disappointed if your Swamp Navigator functions well but looks boring!

Brainstorming

Look carefully at those design features (above) and start asking yourself some questions. For example, What is a swamp? Is a Louisiana swamp different from other swamps? What is the best way to maneuver through water? Make a list of questions and use the Internet to search for answers. But don't get lost while you're surfing the Web. Start with key words that relate to your questions, for example, "Louisiana swamp." Search the Web until all your questions are answered. And make sure that your questions cover all those design features. While you're surfing the Web, think ahead to the presentation you'll be giving.

Sell the Idea
Selling the idea is part of the design challenge. Arturo is your uncle. He'll give you a hard time whether your design is good or bad. BUT if it's going to be built (and you know there's no beach vacation unless it does), then you will have to make your ideas clear to a lot of people.

You'll create a project Web site to get your ideas across. These are the things you must include on your project Web site:

→ Describe the design challenge.
→ Describe your research (the questions you came up with while brainstorming and the answers you found on the Internet).
→ Describe how the mechanics of Arturo's Swamp Navigator satisfy those design challenges.
→ Include plenty of details about those mechanics. In what ways are the mechanics for traveling through water different than for traveling on land? What are the mechanics involved in lifting and moving objects?
→ Be sure to include some interesting stories about swamps. How much swampland is in the United States? What's the most important piece of swampland in the history of the United States? Is Louisiana swampland anything like other swampland? What animals live in swamp lands?

What challenges did you come across while designing and programming the Swamp Navigator?
What research information helped you design and build the Swamp Navigator?

SOURCE: Conexiones website. Available: http://conexiones.asu.edu/summer1999/asu99.html

This project meets the standard for equitable access to resources and technology. The curriculum the project presents is challenging, and it communicates high expectations. A review of student projects shown in the project's Web site demonstrate that students have opportunities for incorporating their own culture into the projects they develop. The student projects also demonstrate creativity and high levels of competence in using technology. The project's focus on professional development helps to ensure that students' home-base schools have information available to them to facilitate students' connections between Conexiones and their regular school programs.

There are migrant programs for secondary migrant students that focus on building competence in skills and strategies that extend beyond academic skills and concepts to such life skills as leadership. The migrant education programs in several states offer summer leadership academies to students in their states. The Migrant Leadership Academy (MLA) sponsored by SHARE is one such program.

MIGRANT LEADERSHIP ACADEMY

Don McBride, a migrant education consultant in the Missouri Migrant Education Program reported that migrant youth have had many opportunities to learn life. Those lessons, however, often do not extend to postsecondary education or to well-paying careers. The MLA, a project that is administered jointly by Missouri, Arkansas, and Oklahoma through a consortium called SHARE, was created to extend the life lessons migrant youth already have learned to include knowledge about postsecondary education and the world of work.

Since the first SHARE MLA was held, in the summer of 1998, the number of participants has grown each year, the anticipated number of participants for the 2001 session being near 100. The MLA is held at a rural Missouri camp that has 150 as its maximum capacity; each state may invite fifty students to be a part of the academy. The three-day summer camp is for migrant youth in grades nine through twelve who come from the three states. Once students have attended a MLA summer session, they are encouraged to attend subsequent sessions, and previous attendance is a priority for selecting participants. The status of "currently migrating" is also a priority for selection, although students who have formerly migrated are selected if there is space.

The goals of the MLA include creating among the participants a vision for and a sense of efficacy about finishing high school and looking beyond to postsecondary education, either college or vocational/technical education. The program of the MLA is aimed at achieving those goals. It includes activities intended to nurture leadership skills and to extend the teaming skills students already have to building productive relationships with new people. There are different foci for the students at different levels. Ninth graders, for example, focus on themselves and their personal abilities; tenth graders look around themselves and at improving their immediate communities. A focus for eleventh and twelfth graders is giving back to their communities. Students also develop physical skills through low and high ropes courses, the high ropes course representing a high personal challenge. A consultant from the University Extension Service, Dr. Jim Wirth, works with the academy participants to assess their own strengths and aptitudes and to match them with potential jobs and careers.

The MLA seeks not only to create in students a vision for post-secondary education and careers; it also provides information about and experience with the cultures of postsecondary education and business. Some of the sessions students attend at the academy focus on such topics as college admission and financial aid. Others focus on how to obtain information from schools and employers, and still others deal with developing skills for interviewing with schools and employers. Academy participants, for example, receive a handbook of information about college admission and financial aid that includes a list of scholarships available specifically for migrant students and Web sites that provide additional information about colleges and financial aid. The MLA also includes a career fair where colleges and businesses set up booths and talk one-to-one with the academy participants.

Between summers, MLA personnel rely on migrant educators in the students' schools to provide ongoing support and connection to the academy. The academy also encourages its participants to participate in the Congressional Award program to continue the work of the academy throughout the school year. The Congressional Award honors students who meet goals they set for themselves in the areas of volunteer public service, personal development, physical fitness, and expedition or exploration. Participants can earn bronze, silver, and gold Congressional Award certificates and medals.

The MLA publishes an annual report about that summer's academy. Academy organizers believe that the goal of helping migrant youth develop leadership skills is being met. According to the 2000 report,

> This year, something powerful took place that validated all our efforts. A rainstorm stymied the Saturday morning outdoor activities: something that we have hoped and prayed would never happen. But this rainstorm caused some of our campers to take leadership in designing and implementing on-the-spot indoor activities that served us until the sun came out and dried things off. It was powerful seeing the leadership development mission of the academy take place before our eyes. We just looked at one another and said, "This is what it's all about!" (SHARE Consortium 2000, 1)

The MLA works to address the standard for high expectations and positive attitudes as it seeks to develop leadership skills that the participants can draw on both in their academic careers and in life. The project helps students identify their own strengths and build on them; at the same time, students build feelings of efficacy. Students also gain metacognitive skills as they negotiate the challenge courses and learn about careers. Participation in the Congressional Award program helps students to make connections between their work in the MLA and their schoolwork; it also helps them to build positive connections to their communities.

Still other programs for migrant students combine academic and personal skills to help the students get back on track to graduate from high school. The Florida Migrant Education Summer Institute identifies migrant students who are at risk of failing and helps them to gain the skills they need to be successful in high school and beyond.

FLORIDA MIGRANT EDUCATION SUMMER INSTITUTE

The Florida Department of Education Office of Migrant Education has administered the Florida Migrant Education Summer Institute every summer since 1985. This project, identified in 1992 as an exemplary migrant education program by the U.S. Department of Education, is a six-week summer residential program that serves at-risk high school migrant students.

The mission of the program is "to provide an exemplary comprehensive residential summer program for eligible secondary migrant student that will increase the student's graduation rate by providing opportunities for credit accrual, promotion, graduation, and continuation of their education at post-secondary institutions. A diverse staff comprised of highly qualified and dedicated professional individuals will offer intensive academic instruction and enriched social, cultural, and technological experiences" (Migrant Education Summer Institute 2000, 1).

The Migrant Education Summer Institute began in 1985 in response to a needs assessment of elementary and secondary migrant students in Pasco County, Florida, conducted in 1984. This needs assessment found that the majority of high school migrant students in Pasco County had high levels of absenteeism, were one or more years older than was appropriate for their grade level in school, and had poor academic achievement. All these factors are known to increase the likelihood that students would either drop out of school before graduating or fail to earn enough credits to graduate even if they stayed in high school for four years. The 1985 pilot program was a day program; it attracted students who were formerly migrant, but it did not attract the students it was intended for, those who were currently migrating and most at risk. An evaluation of the pilot program determined that the design of the program was the problem. Students who were classified as currently migrant migrated with their families; they were not in the area when the program was offered.

The next year, the program was revised to become a residential program. As a residential program, it offered a place for the high school students to stay while their families were migrating and working in another area. The revised program also addressed the issue of the income families would lose while their children were not working by offering a stipend for participation. Another drawback of the original program was that it was remedial and did not offer for-credit courses. The revised program offered courses that could earn credit toward promotion and graduation. The willingness to continually assess the needs of the students the program targets and to adjust the program to meet those needs has characterized the program since its beginning. Glenn Johnston, the program's current director, reports that the program continues to "expand and evolve to meet the challenge of increasing the graduation rate of Florida's at risk migrant students."

The goal of the current program is to "encourage positive values such as good citizenship, self/social responsibility, leadership, self-advocacy, appreciation of diverse populations, and the importance of contributing to the global community." The Florida Migrant Education Summer Institute works toward this goal "through a collaborative partnership with parents, students, district/state personnel, and community agencies in conjunction with post-secondary institutions" (Migrant Education Summer Institute 2000, 3).

Specifically, the program provides comprehensive services that

- Help students obtain credits toward promotion and/or graduation
- Enable students to receive individualized remedial instruction based on documented deficiencies
- Enable limited or non-English-proficient students to improve English communication skills
- Help students improve their grade point averages
- Help students develop the study skills needed to achieve their academic potential

 •• Expose students to career development activities designed to assist them in exploring careers and planning the strategies needed to attain their individual goals
 •• Help students meet their personal, academic, and vocational needs through individual and group counseling
 •• Expose students to activities designed to foster a positive self-concept, leadership skills, and social awareness (Migrant Education Summer Institute 2000, 3)

Students are recommended for participation in the summer institute by their school counselors. Once the recommended students apply to the program, they are selected according to a set of factors that identify applicants most at risk and, therefore, most in need of intervention. The factors include (1) the discrepancy between a student's age and grade placement, (2) the number of moves and school transfers a student has made in the past year, (3) a student's grade point average, (4) whether a student has attempted the High School Competency Test and failed it, (5) a student's failure to accrue credits at a rate that would allow him or her to graduate with peers of the same age, and (6) a student's eligibility for graduation during the summer institute. Using these factors, students are selected, placed on a waiting list, or deemed ineligible. The summer institute particularly targets ninth-grade students who are older than their grade-level peers. Most students identified as ineligible are those who do not qualify for a migrant Certificate of Eligibility.

The summer institute is a six-week residential program housed at the University of South Florida. The program gives students the opportunity to experience college life and to begin to see postsecondary education as a personal possibility. The program is coordinated and administered by the Florida Department of Education with the University of South Florida as fiscal agent.

Staff and student ratios are kept as small as possible to provide the highest level of educational services and counseling. There is one teacher and one residential counselor for every ten students in the program; the guidance counselor ratio is one for every twenty-five students. Program administrators, teachers, guidance counselors, and residential counselors live with the students in the university dormitories.

The Migrant Education Summer Institute has an intensive weekday schedule designed to ensure that students spend enough time in academic classes to earn two academic credits. If they are enrolled in a PASS course at the same time, they can earn an additional half-credit. Guidance counselors from the students' home schools help to select appropriate academic courses for the students. All the courses that are offered are developed from the Florida curriculum frameworks and course code directory standards; they meet the minimum number of clock hours required for earning credit in the state of Florida. The schedule also includes time each day for work on study skills, personal and vocational counseling, and recreation.

Weekday Daily Schedule

7:00 a.m. to 8:00 a.m.	Breakfast
8:00 a.m. to 10:10 a.m.	First period
10:20 a.m. to 12:30 p.m.	Second period
12:30 p.m. to 1:30 p.m.	Lunch
1:40 p.m. to 3:50 p.m.	Third period
4:00 p.m. to 5:00 p.m.	Recreation time
5:00 p.m. to 5:30 p.m.	Shower and clean-up time
5:30 p.m. to 6:30 p.m.	Dinner
6:30 p.m. to 9:00 p.m.	Study skills/career development/tutoring
9:00 p.m. to 10:15 p.m.	Free time
10:30 p.m.	Lights out

The courses students take during the day are for-credit courses. The evening classes provide study skills instruction to help students learn how to learn and to achieve their academic potential, and career development instruction to help students develop individual career plans. Other activities are designed to allow the students to discover and develop their leadership potential, become more socially aware, foster a positive self-concept, and encourage them to become involved in some type of postsecondary education or vocational training. Tutorial assistance is available to students throughout the day, and evening classes help students with academic deficiencies and ensure their successful learning.

All instructors in the Migrant Education Summer Institute are certified teachers in the state of Florida; they all teach classes in the summer institute that are appropriate to their certifications. Class size is kept small enough to allow the teachers the time necessary to determine the specific educational needs of their students and to provide instruction that meets those needs. The residential counselors act as a support group for the instructional staff; they duplicate materials, reserve and deliver audiovisual equipment, and provide tutoring and additional instruction to students.

Guidance counselors meet one-on-one with each student several times during the program to discuss students' strengths, help them develop strategies for meeting graduation requirements, and discuss future careers and career plans. The counselors help each student set short- and long-term goals and strategies to meet those goals, and to make an Individualized Plan of Action (IPA). At the end of the summer institute, the IPAs are forwarded to the students' counselors in their home districts to help the educators there provide the continuity of services between the summer institute and the students' home schools that is so critical for these migrant students.

Residential counselors are involved in the instructional program and the guidance program. They monitor the academic progress of the students and they serve as tutors during the day and evening classes. The residential counselors also serve as models to the students; many of them are former participants in the summer institute. In addition, they are responsible for ensuring the students eat properly and get plenty of exercise and rest.

In study skills classes, students are tested to determine their learning style profiles and to help them understand their own learning strengths and needs. They are taught a variety of study skills, including what, how, when, and where to study; how to read and extract information from content text; and how to research and write a paper. Basically, the student skills classes focus on learning how they learn best and how to use this knowledge to continue to learn.

The summer institute includes career exploration and development. This component of the program begins with an assessment of personality, needs, interests, skills, and attitudes to help each student create a personal profile that can serve as the basis for guidance toward appropriate and viable career paths. Students have opportunities to learn about careers that align with their personal profiles. This career learning includes information about training and education requirements for the careers, as well as the kinds of skills the careers require. In this component of the summer institute, students also learn how to read classified advertisements, how to complete job applications, how to develop resumes, and how to interview successfully. To help them practice the interview skills and strategies they learn, students have opportunities to participate in mock interviews conducted by professionals in the fields in which the students are interested. This component also provides students with information about colleges and other postsecondary education, including information about admissions and financial aid.

Guest speakers visit the program each week. These guests support the goals of the guidance component as they speak to the program participants about a variety of motivational topics, including the advantages of staying in school; drug, alcohol, and tobacco abuse prevention; setting goals for college or vocational education; and positive self-image. Most of the speakers also serve as role models for the students because they are former migrants themselves. For example, during the 2000 summer institute, one of the guest speakers was an assistant principal at one of the largest high schools in Hillsborough County. That person had not only been a migrant; he had been a participant in the Migrant Education Summer Institute. He had also served as a residential counselor, then as a residential supervisor, and later as the assistant director of the summer institute.

Students are in residence at the University of South Florida seven days a week during the six-week program. Weekends offer a break from the intense routine of the weekday schedule; they are reserved for an expanded schedule of organized recreational activities that are aimed at helping students meet the goals of the program. Students take field trips to sites that are positive and memorable, as well as fun and educational; trips might take students to the Museum of Science and Industry in Fort Lauderdale, Busch Gardens, historical sites, aquariums, science exhibits, and so on. Students go to the beach and they have opportunities for such recreational activities as canoeing. The trips are designed to expand students' horizons and offer them new experiences.

Each summer, students at the institute are expected to participate in an Olympic competition. Many migrant students do not have the opportunity to participate in sports programs or teams at their high schools because of eligibility requirements or because they do not stay in a school long enough. The Olympic competition offers students the opportunity for athletic competition. The events in the Olympic competition are designed to build teamwork, sportsmanship, and self-esteem. All students are required to enter at least one of the offered events, which include such sports as swimming, track, softball, basketball, volleyball, basketball, and soccer. Gold, silver, and bronze medals are awarded for each of the Olympic competition events.

One of the ways that students develop leadership through the summer institute is through student government. Student government elections are one of the first activities students engage in at the summer institute. To run for office in the student government, students must collect signatures and file petitions. They define election platforms and develop campaign materials such as posters and speeches. The county supports the student government by printing real ballots, allowing the summer institute to use real voting machines for the elections, and counting the ballots. Student government officers are responsible for planning and organizing some of the student activities. They also plan community service projects for the summer institute.

Community service is an opportunity for students to give back to the community. In the past, students have visited Shriners, veterans, and cancer hospitals, as well as retirement homes and elementary schools. They have raised money through car washes and by donating a portion of the stipends they earn through the program. Students in several summer institutes together raised enough money to fund a four-year scholarship for a small migrant boy who had lost his right arm in a farming accident.

At every summer institute students present a talent show. An enriching experience, the talent show supports the Migrant Education Summer Institute goal of helping students develop positive self-concept. Students have the opportunity through the talent show to demonstrate their nonacademic talents. The director of the summer institute noted that the talent show also offers the opportunity for other students and for program staff to view students in a whole new light.

Every year, through the Migrant Education Summer Institute, some students complete the requirements for graduation. For them, the summer institute provides a graduation ceremony and celebration. Each graduate gives a short speech, and diplomas from students' home schools are awarded. Most of the principals of those home schools attend the graduation ceremony to award the diplomas in person. The University of South Florida supports the graduation by sponsoring a graduation dance for these graduating seniors. The graduation ceremony and celebration serve as reminders to other students in the program that graduation is a goal that they can all reach.

In the summer of 2000, the Florida Migrant Education Summer Institute served 140 students drawn from a twenty-seven county area. Of those students, 138 completed the program. All but one of those who completed the program earned credit toward promotion or graduation. All the students who completed the program improved their grade point averages. All but one who had the potential to meet graduation requirements by the end of the summer institute actually graduated. And of the students who took the Florida High School Competency Test, all either improved their test scores or passed the test. Students who participate in this program have a rate of graduation that is nearly twice that of migrant high school students nationwide.

Several Florida colleges and universities, among them the University of South Florida and Stetson University, have offered scholarships to Migrant Education Summer Institute graduates. Most of the scholarships awarded to these students are full four-year scholarships. The program boasts many graduates and former participants who are now successful professionals, including former students who work in the program. The director noted that the former students who are teachers and residential counselors in the program have a special understanding of the migrant experience and a special empathy for the students in the program.

In 2001, the Migrant Education Summer Institute will serve 150 students, an increase of ten students over the previous year. The director noted that in past years, the program was larger; it was offered at multiple sites each summer and even more students were given an educational boost. A decrease in funding led to reducing the size of the program; summer institute personnel are looking for funds to be able to provide this opportunity to more students. Besides increasing the number of students in 2001, the Migrant Education Summer Institute will also begin to offer students the opportunity to earn additional high school and even college credits through taking the College Level Examination Program (CLEP) tests.

Since 1992, the Florida Migrant Education Summer Institute Program has been recognized by the U.S. Department of Education as an exemplary program. In 1992, the program was one of six migrant education programs to receive the U.S. Department of Education's National Exemplary Program Award for Excellence in Migrant Education.

The Florida Migrant Education Summer Institute is aimed at extending its participants' opportunities to learn, both in the summer program and in the students' own high schools. This program addresses migrant students' unique needs by providing housing while parents are migrating. It helps students to learn how to learn and to monitor their own learning, addressing not only academics, but also metacognition and self-esteem. In providing staff who are former migrants themselves, the program creates an environment that respects and builds on students' own experiences and values. The efforts of the program to coordinate with students' home-base high schools through communicating the IPAs and transferring academic information demonstrate the shared responsibility of the institute and the home-base high schools for the instruction, assessment, and success of the students.

All these programs demonstrate how states, school districts, and schools have created innovative responses to the particular and unique needs of migrant children and youth. In many ways they meet the NASDME standards for equity, as well as DiCerbo's recommendations for effective instruction in migrant education programs. These are only a few of the many programs that supplement regular educational programs to provide the extra supports that migrant students need to overcome the barriers that their migrant lifestyle presents. There are many more innovative programs and projects going on, and many, many educators are dedicated to helping migrant students achieve academically, personally, and economically. Chapter 6 describes a program that has applied these standards and recommendations not only to supplemental programs but to their migrant students' entire academic experience.

REFERENCES

Arnold, L. "Kusko Book Express Anchors Third Season." *Elicaq* (fall 2000): 10.

Best S.E.L.F. *Creating the Masterpiece.* Mount Vernon, WA: Elite Productions, 1999.

———. *Skagit and Yakima Counties Best S.E.L.F.* Mount Vernon, WA: Elite Productions, 2001.

Conexiones. *Summer 1999.* Tempe, AZ: Conexiones, 1999. Available: http://conexiones.asu.edu/summer1999/asu99.html

———. *The Conexiones Project.* Tempe, AZ: Conexiones, 2001. Available: http://conexiones.asu.edu

DiCerbo, P. A. "Why Migrant Education Matters." *Issue & Brief No. 8.* Washington, DC: National Clearinghouse for Bilingual Education Center for the Study of Language & Education, 2001. Available: http://www/ncbe.gwu.edu

★Estrella. *Estupendas Laptop Talk,* 2000. Available: http://www.estrella.org/newsletter.htm

———. *Description,* 2001a. Available: http://www.estrella.org/description. htm

———. *Identification,* 2001b. Available: http://www.estrella.org/identification. htm

———. *Mentors,* 2001c. Available: http://www.estrella.org/mentors.htm

———. *NovaNET,* 2001d. Available: http://www.estrella.org/novanet.htm

———. *Parents,* 2001e. Available: http://www.estrella.org/parents.htm

Hansen, W. *Best S.E.L.F.: An Advocate Program of Excellence for Children. Replication Manual.* Mount Vernon, WA: Best S.E.L.F. Program, 1999.

"*Harvest of Hope:* Staging the Migrant Experience in a Classic Theatrical Setting." In *35 Years of Harvesting Dreams and Launching Futures.* Program booklet of the 2001 National Migrant Education Conference, Orlando, Florida, April 10, 2001.

Kindler, A. *Education of Migrant Children in the United States.* Washington, DC: National Clearinghouse for Bilingual Education, 1995.

Menchaco, V. D., and J. A. Ruiz-Escalente. *Instructional Strategies for Migrant Students.* Charleston, WV: ERIC Clearinghouse on Rural Education and Small Schools, 1995. (ERIC Document No. RC-95–10)

Migrant Education Summer Institute. Handout prepared for the National Association of State Directors of Migrant Education (NASDME) annual conference, Orlando, Florida, April 2000.

National Association of State Directors of Migrant Education (NASDME). *Giving*

Migrant Students an Opportunity to Learn. Sunnyside, WA: National Association of Migrant Educators, 1994.

Putnam County Educational Service Center. *Summary of the HOSTS Pilot Project, Putnam County Summer Migrant Education, Summer 2000.* Unpublished report presented at the National Migrant Education Conference, Orlando, Florida, April, 2000.

Romo, H. D. *Reaching Out: Best Practices for Educating Mexican-Origin Children and Youth.* Charleston, WV: ERIC Clearinghouse on Rural Education and Small Schools, 1999.

Sealts, A. "Students Making Academic Gains." *Putnam County Sentinel,* August 2, 2000.

SHARE Consortium. *Migrant Leadership Academy: Academy 2000 Report.* Monett, MO: SHARE Consortium, 2000.

Sutton, E. *Knowing and Teaching the Migrant Child.* Washington, DC: National Education Association, 1960.

———. *2000–2001 Exemplary Migrant Students.* Austin, TX: University of Texas at Austin Distance Education Center, 2000a.

———. "Migrant Student Program." *Discovery: Research and Scholarship at the University of Texas at Austin* 15, no. 4 (2000b): 31–33.

Chapter Six

ᴥ Putting it All Together: Net-TLC+

Chapter 5 described programs that meet the National Association of State Directors of Migrant Education standards for equity and DiCerbo's recommendations for effective migrant programs. The programs are innovative, and they provide opportunities for migrant children and youth to be successful. Because the funding for migrant education programs is small and represents only a very small percentage of the funding in any school district, the vast majority of these migrant education programs operate on a small scale.

This chapter tells the story of a migrant education program in Colorado that is aiming to level the playing field for migrant children, youth, and families through collaboration across school districts and federal, state, and local programs, as well as community organizations. This program is value-added, that is, much more than the sum of its parts. Through the use of Internet-based technology, the Board of Cooperative Education Services (Centennial BOCES) Office of Compensatory Education (Colorado) has worked to bring together many federal, state, and local programs and projects into a comprehensive effort to address the needs and enhance the educational access and achievement of the migrant children and families that are served by the school districts in the region.

A middle school teacher who has been involved in this work described the value of this work for her and for her students:

> There have been several times that having the Internet in my classroom has been a real savior. It has been invaluable for several of my monolingual Spanish-speaking students. We have used it to do research when nothing else has been available.
>
> Our school has an average size middle school library. As one would imagine, we have many materials in Spanish but not covering every topic the students are required to research. I have helped one of my eighth-grade students, Abby, with materials in Spanish this year that I have never before had available to me.

> With the use of the Internet there are no limits to the topics we can research. We researched gazelles and the rain forest for sixth graders, we research obscure minerals for seventh-grade science, and Native Americans and the Mexican conquests for eighth-grade history. Abby had to do a report of the Anasazi Indians for U.S. history and the information in our library was limited, and entirely in English. . . .
>
> We were able to find many sources on the Internet for her to use. The amazing thing about the Internet was that everything we found could automatically be translated into Spanish with the push of a button. Abby was able to find pictures and text that she could understand. The best part was that she had the exact same articles in Spanish and English so she could compare them and add to her second language acquisition. Once she learned the power of the Internet, there was no stopping her. . . .
>
> Abby is exactly the kind of student that needs exposure to technology. . . . The Internet has helped Abby achieve a level of success that was unimaginable! (Centennial BOCES 2001a, 19)

The Centennial BOCES Office of Compensatory Education in Greeley, Colorado, administers and coordinates federally funded education programs in fourteen school districts in the state. These districts cover an area of about 40,000 square miles in north central Colorado, roughly from Fort Lupton in the south to the Wyoming state line in the north, and from Fort Morgan in the east to the Estes Park area on the west.

The region serves about 6,000 migrant students every school year, about 4,000 of them being served during the school year, and about 2,000 during the summer. Approximately 10 percent (667 in March 2001) of the year-round migrant population of the area come from Mexico.

The mission of the Centennial BOCES is "to provide high-quality programs and services through collaboration which supports the educational priorities of member districts and enriches educational opportunities for students" (Centennial BOCES n.d., 1). Not only is there a collaborative of school districts in the Centennial BOCES; the BOCES also works to connect programs so that all students in the member districts receive appropriate services without duplication.

COORDINATING PROGRAMS TO ADD VALUE

The Office of Compensatory Education of the Centennial BOCES administers a number of federal compensatory education programs, state programs, and local programs, all of which address the needs of migrant children, youth, and their families. The federal programs include Title I Part A, Title I Part C (the Migrant Education Program), Title VII (the Systemwide Bilingual Project), Title IV (Safe and Drug-Free Schools and Communities), Title VI (Improving America's Schools through Innovative Education), Title VI-D (Class Size Reduction), the Migrant Education Even Start (MEES), Goals 2000, and Reading Is Fundamental (RIF). State programs administered by the Centennial BOCES include the Colorado English Language Proficiency Act (ELPA) Program and a Colorado Technology Literacy Challenge Fund Grant. The office also administers a grant from the private Denver Hill Foundation.

Administering all these programs through one regional office provides efficiency of scale; administrative costs are considerably lower than if each participating school district administered each of these programs individually. Lower administrative costs allow the BOCES to spend much more of the funding directly on providing services to students. Administering the programs centrally also allows the BOCES to operate programs that small school districts would not have either financial or personnel resources to support and/or maintain.

Each of the programs contributes components that serve as part of the BOCES' mission of enriching educational opportunities for students. The brochure for the Centennial BOCES Office of Compensatory Education program describes how each of the programs in the region is implemented.

Basic Title I

The Title I, Part A program (basic Title I) provides supplemental educational services in reading, language arts, and mathematics, as well as support services in guidance, social work, and health and nutrition to elementary and secondary students. This program also includes a strong parent involvement initiative; parents are involved in project planning and evaluation, parent-teacher conferences, Title I conferences, workshops, and meetings. Schools in the region provide Title I service through one of "two major types of educational settings" (Centennial BOCES 2001a, 3). In some schools and classrooms, Title I teachers or teacher assistants provide additional instruction in students' regular classrooms; in others, students leave their regular classrooms for this supplemental instruction. Still other schools and classrooms offer a combination of in-class and pull-out instruction.

Title I Migrant

The Migrant Education Program has the basic aim of supplementing the migrant child's regular education with services that meet the child's unique educational needs that result from moving from school district to school district. Under the Migrant Education Program, the service provided to children in the Centennial BOCES include regular school year and summer programs in reading, mathematics, language arts, and the functional use of English; identification and recruitment of migrant students in the fourteen school districts that are in Colorado's Region I; distance learning for high school students and adults through the University of Texas at Austin; staff development for migrant and ESL teachers; parent involvement; a Summer Food Service grant providing breakfast, lunch, and snacks to summer school program students; and summer medical/health services and dental screenings.

Mary Ellen Good, the Migrant Education Program coordinator, reported in an interview with the author on April 2, 2001, that each of the program's five recruiters works in one area of the region to identify and recruit migrant families as soon as they arrive in the area. The team, which meets weekly, has established relationships with area employers, businesses, and community agencies and organizations, both for purposes of recruiting and to help migrant families access the resources they need. A relationship with the Lions Club, for example, has resulted in holding regular comprehensive vision clinics for migrant students and their families that not only offer vision screenings but also provide frames and correctional lenses to them on the spot at no cost. Two migrant health centers are in the region and are served by the Centennial BOCES; these centers provide summer dental and medical care and routine vision and hearing screenings.

Title VII—Systemwide Improvement Project

The 2000–2001 school year is the sixth year of the BOCES' implementation of a Title VII Systemwide Improvement Project. This project is designed to meet the needs of about 1,500 Limited English Proficient (LEP) students in five of the school districts served by the Centennial BOCES. Between 25 and 48 percent of the student populations of these school districts are English-language learners who qualify for English as a Second Language (ESL) instruction. In the first year of the project, the grant funded two ESL teachers to work with the students in each district. Besides these direct services to students, a major component of this project is professional development. There is a shortage of qualified ESL and bilingual teachers nationally; the project is aimed at addressing that shortage by helping teachers already in the schools to become ESL-endorsed bilingual teachers. The grant provides professional development for school personnel in several forms. Scholarships are provided through this project for teachers to enroll in coursework that leads to endorsement or certification as bilingual teachers.

Creating an optimum learning environment for English-language learners requires more than hiring or training a few ESL or bilingual teachers. The responsibility for these students' learning lies with all staff members of these schools. Under the grant, all the teachers have had professional development in "sheltered English" instruction. In addition, they have participated in professional development to help them understand and be sensitive to the cultural backgrounds and needs of English-language learners in their classrooms. To communicate that their participation in the professional development was valued, teachers were awarded three semester hours of graduate credit for their work.

Administrators also participate in professional development to equip them to be instructional leaders in English-language learning, to coach and provide feedback to the teachers in their schools, to evaluate classroom teachers and bilingual teachers as they work with English-language learners, and to judge the quality of the bilingual education programs in their schools. Also earning three semester hours of graduate credit for their work, administrators developed a teacher evaluation instrument through the professional development coursework that reflects what they have learned about the effective teaching of English-language learners.

Another component of the project is the provision of a parent coordinator who provides training for parents and works to involve parents more actively in their children's schools. This project also works to build business partnerships and community support for these programs.

Title IV—Safe and Drug-Free Schools and Communities

The Title IV Safe and Drug-Free Schools and Communities program provides opportunities for tobacco, drug, and safety education, and awareness for all students. The grant also sponsors school events that support safe and drug-free schools and communities. The Office of Compensatory Education also acts as a broker for the school districts it serves, informing them of additional grants and other funding, as well as of conferences and workshops available to them.

Title VI—Improving America's Schools through Innovative Education

Title VI, Improving America's Schools through Innovative Education, is designed to help teachers acquire knowledge and skill in implementing innovative practices in their classrooms, particularly those related to the use of technology, and in having the materials available to do so. This project provides materials to upgrade school libraries, as well as supplementary classroom print and nonprint, video, and audio materials. The grant also supports the purchase of computers for schools, supplies teachers within school districts to set up the computers, and trains teachers and students on the computer systems and how to use them to enhance teaching and assessment.

Title VI-D—Class Size Reduction

Title VI-D is a federal initiative to reduce class size in kindergarten through third-grade classrooms. Through this initiative, the Centennial BOCES Office of Compensatory Education helps school districts with recruiting and hiring teachers and with professional development that helps teachers learn how to maximize instructional opportunities in smaller classes through individual and small group instruction. Three of the school districts served by the Centennial BOCES are too small to receive enough money to hire additional teachers; the funds were used instead for professional development to better meet the needs of young children in their schools.

Migrant Education Even Start

The Centennial BOCES Office of Compensatory Education Migrant Education Even Start (MEES) employs a statewide coordinator to coordinate the MEES program and offers migrant education programs in twelve local school districts across Colorado. Other partners in the Colorado Statewide MEES Consortium include the Colorado Department of Education, Office of Migrant Education, and Colorado Even Start.

The MEES program is designed

> •• To increase opportunities for migratory parents of a child aged birth through three years to be the child's first teacher by providing timely information about the child's growth and development and using home visits and the Parents As Teachers program

•• To provide parents with opportunities to increase life management, literacy, employment, and self-advocacy skills to interact effectively within a community and to exercise their rights and responsibilities as citizens (Net-TLC+ 2001)

To meet those goals, MEES provides educational services for migrant families that includes adult literacy, early childhood education, parenting education, and professional development for MEES personnel. The MEES program in Colorado uses the Parents As Teachers model to provide home-based educational services to families. The program has twelve parent educators who regularly visit migrant families to provide early childhood and parenting education and to help migrant parents access adult education and literacy services. Each of the parent educators works with eighteen families; about 215 families are served by MEES.

Reading Is Fundamental

Reading Is Fundamental (RIF) helps families and communities prepare young children for reading and motivate children to read by providing books for them to keep; migrant children often possess few books or other print materials of their own. For migrant programs, RIF waives the usual requirement for matching funds from a school or school district. Through more than $6,500 provided by RIF, the Centennial BOCES Office of Compensatory Education coordinates with schools to purchase books and distribute them to migrant children at five family events held each year.

English-Language Proficiency Act

The Colorado English Language Proficiency Act (ELPA) coordinates with the Migrant Education Program and the programs offered through Title VII to offer direct instructional services to English-language learners. It also provides support for and collaboration with classroom teachers who work with English-language learners. Funds are reallocated to school districts to support English-language proficiency programs based on how many LEP students are enrolled in the schools. The funding is provided for each English-language learner for two years.

The Hill Foundation

The Colorado Migrant Education Program has a grant from the private Denver Hill Foundation to support the teaching of reading in the Migrant Education Program. This grant supports the purchase of books, reading activity games, and instructional materials for teaching reading in the Migrant Education Program in the state. The Centennial BOCES Office of Compensatory Education uses the grant to provide print materials for migrant parents. These include Spanish-English dictionaries and fiction and nonfiction books in Spanish.

Net-TLC+/ Colorado Technology Literacy Challenge Fund Grant

Through cutting-edge technology, the Centennial BOCES Office of Compensatory Education has been able to enhance and extend all the services provided through the programs and projects already described. In 1997, the Centennial BOCES was awarded a grant by the Colorado Department of Education through GOALS 2000 to implement Networks in Technology as Learning Communities (Net-TLC+ 2001).

Based on the success of its original Net-TLC project, the Centennial BOCES extended and expanded its original plan to create Net-TLC+, whose goal is "to implement standards and close the achievement gap of students who traditionally do poorly on assessments [including migrant students], are at risk of not meeting state or local content standards, have limited proficiency in English and are educationally disadvantaged" (Centennial BOCES n.d., 3).

Net-TLC+ uses leveraged resources from community and business partners, state and regional technical assistance providers, and universities to move educators forward with educational change. Its goal is to improve teaching and student learning by using technology as a tool for professional development to carry out standards-based instruction (Centennial BOCES n.d, 1).

Net-TLC+ uses as its vehicle an Internet-based interactive Web site at www.Net-TLC.org. This Web site was developed as a framework for three interactive networks, through which support for teachers, students, and the community is provided. These three networks, the Teacher Network (T-Net), the Learner Network (L-Net), and the Community Network (C-Net), were designed to link the greater community of learners that make up the constituency of the Centennial BOCES.

The Centennial BOCES partnered with Dream Team Technologies in Denver in 1997 to develop the Net-TLC Web site. Dream Team Technologies reports that the site "allows teachers to participate in real-time conversations with on-line coaches, have their own e-mail accounts to communicate with other ESL teachers, and have on-line meetings in a virtual conference room. It also provides the means for implementing Professional Development Plans and for incorporating standards into curricula" (Dream Team Technologies 1999,1).

A fourth network, A-Net, for administrators, was added when the project became Net-TLC+; the Centennial BOCES secured additional funding for the project in its second year in the form of a grant from the Colorado Technology Literacy Challenge Fund. Net-TLC, which began with thirty-three teachers, expanded in its second year as Net-TLC+ to include sixty-nine teachers and six principals. This network of sixty-nine teachers now forms a key link in professional development in the eleven school districts that are part of this project.

As evidence of the Centennial BOCES ongoing assessment of the needs of that greater community of learners, a fifth network has most recently been added to Net-TLC+. In a conversation with the author on April 2, 2001, Margaret Walpole, the director of compensatory education at the Centennial BOCES, identified the need of students to have immediate access to caring, concerned adults in the form of counseling. Net-TLC+ added cyber counseling in the form of Cyber Counseling Net to provide counseling to students whenever they need it.

The Net-TLC+ Web site includes several components, all of which are aimed at the project's goals:

- To support professional development for teachers and administrators through the use of technology
- To help establish communication networks between teachers, administrators, and resource persons
- To provide avenues for teachers to plan lessons
- To give students the tools to learn (Centennial BOCES Net-TLC+ Project Brochure, n.d.)

The components of the Web site are an events calendar; a personalized home page for each participant; individual journals, time sheets, and professional development plans; Internet Web links organized by school level, including the Colorado state standards and the ESL standards; a directory of all Net-TLC+ members; a bulletin board and chat rooms for ongoing discussions; e-mail accounts for each Net-TLC+ member; a list of forms project members use for the formal professional development part of the project; video viewing of the Net-TLC+ professional development events; and handouts and materials from the events in downloadable format.

According to the Net-TLC+ brochure, the Teacher Net (T-Net) was designed as a tool for delivering professional development with the goal of improving student achievement. With the T-Net, teachers are provided opportunities to "share resources, ask and receive answers to questions, gather knowledge about effective teaching practices, and interact with other teachers and mentors" (Net-TLC+ 2001). It also offers opportunities for teachers to use technology as a tool for their own instruction.

As teachers join the Net-TLC+ network, they are assigned cyber coaches, or mentors, who coach teachers in the use of Net-TLC+ and guide them in developing personal professional development plans (PDPs) that include continuing education, curriculum and instruction, assessment, using technology for themselves and integrating it into their classroom instruction, and parent involvement. Cyber coaches then serve as guides "through collaboration, inquiry, and reflective practice. Net-TLC+ educators and their coaches set objectives, [identify] professional development resources, and systematically [carry] out the PDPs" (Centennial BOCES 2001a, 1). The cyber coaches who coach teachers in the Net-TLC+ project have a variety of expertise and backgrounds. The coaches are drawn from the nationwide community of educators and "assist teachers by generating discussion, asking questions, providing resources, and offering suggestions and advice." Some of the topics they address with teachers include bilingual education and ESL, using technology in the classroom, aligning instruction and assessment, teaching strategies, and increasing student achievement (Centennial BOCES Net-TLC+ Project Brochure, n.d.).

Professional development provided through Net-TLC+ includes using electronic journals and threaded e-mail discussions on standards-based instruction as well as more traditional face-to-face professional development that includes workshops and a summer institute.

By the first year of the project, professional development was well established, ongoing, and comprehensive: "Educators and coaches spent one-half day monthly on professional development activities. . . . Teachers and coaches were responsible for posing e-mail network problem-based inquiries to support communication, interaction, and professional development. Each day, educators spent thirty minutes in e-mail discussion sharing effective instructional strategies about standards-based curriculum and instruction to promote student achievement" (Centennial BOCES 2001a, 1).

The T-Net includes a calendar of professional development activities. For the 2000–2001 school year, the calendar includes workshops for Title I, ESL, and Net-TLC+. Topics for ESL, for example, include "Integrating Sheltered Content" and "Sheltering Literacy." Net-TLC+ professional development is centered on using technology in the classroom, including digital imagery, Power Point, Web site development, and visual/technology curriculum enhancement.

The T-Net, in addition to the calendar, provides descriptions of training opportunities for teachers. One such page lists dates, school levels, and presenters for a series of week-long summer sheltered English workshops. Another page allows teachers to place requests for training in specific technology topics, such as digital camera and building your own Web site. Another page, titled "Kathi's Corner," includes information about what's new on T-Net and provides links to Internet resources for teachers. A recent page on "Kathi's Corner" included sites that provide information about high-stakes testing, "Camp Yahoo en Español" (Yahoo's Spanish-language Internet education initiative), a Web site that will translate documents from English to Spanish, and a directory of national fellowships, internships, and scholarships for Latino youth. Kathi Van Soest, the Centennial BOCES program coordinator for Net-TLC+ and Professional Development, reported that this page is regularly updated to provide the latest information to teachers.

Teachers have opportunities through T-Net to participate in ongoing, online threaded discussions that have the potential to become one-on-one professional development. This format offers a safe place where teachers can share real issues without fearing that those issues will affect the teachers' relationships within their own schools or become part of their teaching evaluations. One such discussion began when a teacher posed a problem he was encountering with the inclusion of a special needs child in his dual bilingual class and asked other teachers to share their experiences with similar situations:

> Hi, everyone: I have a concern. I work in a dual bilingual immersion setting K–2. In one of the classes, there is a student who has Down's Syndrome. He is a beautiful child, full of peace and love. My problem is that while he is in my reading class very little can get done because the student is walking around interacting with other students and objects in the class. My group can't pay attention to me and the child so there is the problem. What are your experiences with inclusion? Do you have any suggestions? Many thanks. P. (Net-TLC+ 2001)

A special education teacher from another dual-language school responded to P.'s concern and questions the next day.

> Many teachers are struggling with ways to support students with disabilities in the general education classroom. Sounds like your student needs a couple of things. First, if he needs to be able to move around, you can allow that, but also put some constraints on it. You could designate an area for movement by taping a line or circle on the floor and

teaching the student to move only within that area. The student probably needs extra attention, too, so be careful to put the area where he
can check in with you, but as much as possible away from the other
students when interaction is not desired. Also, the student should be
provided with modified work so that he will be better able to work independently and so disrupt less. You should have support from the
special education teacher for some of this. An appropriate use of pull-
out is to teach a child specific tasks that the child can then do independently in the regular classroom. The special ed teacher can help you
modify work if you plan ahead and find a time to meet and discuss the
lessons you want to teach. L. (Net-TLC+ 2001)

This special education teacher's response began by reassuring the regular classroom teacher that he was not alone in dealing with this issue.
She went on to offer specific strategies for him to try, both with the child
and in working with the special education teacher in his building, to obtain the appropriate assistance for this special needs child.

In his response to L., P. provided more information about the
strategies he had already tried with this particular student, as well as
some insight into his level of frustration. He also described his willingness to learn and to try new strategies:

I tried allowing the child movement, but there's no way to restrict that
movement because the child doesn't understand limits. What happens
is that the kids go get the student before they get out the door. The special ed teacher in our building is overwhelmed at this point in time as
there are so many students needing her attention. At the moment, I get
fifteen minutes of her time in the morning. She hopes to have someone
on board soon, but who knows when this will actually happen. The
child responds in ways that reflect the development of an eighteen-
month-old. I am feeling bad about not providing the very best for the
child but at the same time I am doing the very best I know how with
the limits of my knowledge. If it would [be] adequate to modify my instruction with a few changes [I would] but this child isn't anywhere
near the work we are doing. I feel like I am being difficult but this is just
my truth for now. As someone said, "I reserve the right to learn more
and do better" and that is what I am doing here. Thanks so much for
time on this issue. P. (Net-TLC+ 2001)

P.'s response indicated that he knew he had found a listening ear, someone who would listen to and acknowledge his frustration; at the same
time, here was someone to whom he could admit to what he viewed as

the "limits of [his] knowledge." For him, the T-Net was a safe, nonthreatening place to look for assistance.

The special education teacher responded by placing much of the responsibility on the special education teacher in P.'s school. She also offered more specific suggestions for working with the student in the regular classroom as well as suggestions that P. could make to the special education teacher at his school.

> P. Every special ed teacher is overwhelmed. Still, some quick and intensive training could help the student function better in your classroom. Is the help the teacher is looking for a paraprofessional or another sp. ed. teacher? What would that person's role be? Have you tried simple things that work with eighteen-month-olds, like holding the child in your lap and having simple manipulative toys available? You should discuss with the special ed teacher what the priority is for the time he/she has to provide support. Should the time be spent working individually with the student in the classroom to do some behavior modification using a reward system? Should it be spent developing tasks for the student which would be more engaging and reduce interruptions? It sounds like you could really use some more support. I hope you get another person soon. L.(Net-TLC+ 2001)

P. wrote back to L., describing how he had used some of the strategies that L. suggested. In his message, he indicated that the strategies had been partially successful.

> Thanks again, L. The child was on my lap much of the time but then bored quickly and looks for something else to do. The manipulatives was a great idea. I got some toys, not small enough to swallow, and set them down on a specific area identified by a blanket I asked the parents to bring from home. Where I am right now with that is that unless someone else is playing with the child it is hard to stay engaged alone. (Net-TLC+ 2001)

It is obvious that P. perceives L. to be a source of ongoing assistance, exactly what teachers need to address the problems and issues they face in their classrooms. The potential of T-Net to support such assistance makes it an effective vehicle for the exchanges of professional knowledge so important to teachers' continuing professional development and to their meeting the educational needs of each child in their classrooms.

Another feature of the T-Net is online professional development. Ms. Van Soest explained that although the Centennial BOCES offers

many opportunities for face-to-face professional development, sometimes it is not possible for teachers to attend. Each of the face-to-face
professional development sessions is now videotaped, and the videos are
available for teachers to access online. A review of the "Online Trainings"
page on the T-Net shows that it provides links to videos of such professional development as a "Coaches Retreat," held in the summer of 2000,
that "yielded two new training sessions. One is a training overview of this
[Net-TLC+] Web site and the other is what to expect as a coach and how
to handle situations." Other listings on the page include "Internet Safety,"
"Hyperstudio Training," and "Introduction to the Palace." Clicking on the
button provided for each video allows the videos to be viewed.

The Palace is a feature of the T-Net that allows teachers to chat in
a variety of formats in real time. Users can navigate to and through the
various rooms of the Palace. Each room offers specific services or a particular format. An auditorium, for example, offers users technical support and customer service. A seminar room allows real-time chat among
several T-Net users, and a locked room allows private chat between two
or more identified individuals. The locked room provides the opportunity for users to discuss information of a sensitive or confidential nature
without having to worry about being "overheard."

A calendar that shows the professional development activities
month by month is another component of the T-Net. Each event on the
calendar links to a description of the event and an application. For Tuesday, April 10, 2001, for example, a workshop, "Using Powerpoint in
Classrooms" was scheduled. Clicking on the workshop title takes the
user to the following description:

Net-TLC+ Training: Using Power Point in Classrooms
Tuesday, April 10, 2001
Notes: This is the third class in a series of three. Participants will show what
they have done with their individual Power Point Presentations to the class.
This class is taught by R. B., 7th grade science teacher at Eaton Middle School.

April 10, 2001
Start Time: Tuesday, 4:30 p.m.
End Time: Tuesday, 7:30 p.m.
Location: Eaton Middle School

Buttons provided with this description allow the user to request
an e-mail reminder of the event a day before it occurs, to link to
Yahoo!Maps to see and be able to print a map of the workshop location,
and to return to the calendar of professional development activities.

Teachers describe the Net-TLC+ project as the support they need to use technology in their classrooms. According to one high school teacher,

> The Net-TLC+ project has trained me to access and take advantage of the world of information available to teachers and students on the Internet. It has also given me the possibility of exchanging information, experiences and ideas with my colleagues in the BOCES school districts. I have learned about new teaching methods, resources, and materials and how to use them. Because of Net-TLC+, I am better informed and better able to deliver effective, up-to-date lessons to my students, and I no longer feel alone and forgotten in my classroom. Now I feel like I'm part of a modern, efficient, and competent group of professionals who are working together to produce better results. (Centennial BOCES 2001a, 6)

The second network in Net-TLC+ is the Learner Net (L-Net). The Net-TLC+ brochure reports that "the L-Net was designed to allow students to build their own Web sites and link them to other students' Web sites, search for and explore information, collaborate with other students on projects, and master the technology of the Internet" (Centennial BOCES Net-TLC+ Project Brochure, n.d.). Through the L-Net, students can also access online learning resources and assessments. The L-Net includes such features as "interactive language games in which students can learn and interact with other students across the country; mentorship training for students . . .; filtering software allowing student access only to acceptable websites; [and] website development tools" (Centennial BOCES Net-TLC+ Project Brochure, n.d.).

On the L-Net, there are buttons for elementary, middle, and high school students "with links to information on hobbies, projects, authors, courses, and current events" (Centennial BOCES 2001a, 2). Migrant students of high school age can link directly to the University of Texas at Austin (UT Austin); L-Net allows these migrant students to choose the high school courses they need to complete and then to register for those courses online. When UT Austin has developed online courses, students will be able to access those courses through L-Net. UT Austin's high school migrant education program is described in more detail in Chapter 5.

The latest addition to the L-Net Web site, and to the Net-TLC+ project, is Cyber Counseling Net, which offers online counseling to students. Through Cyber Counseling Net, students in the participating schools have access to licensed, caring school counselors. The Web site enables students to conduct private, secure conversations at convenient times. The online counselors, many of whom are bilingual, listen to students' concerns and offer advice when appropriate. The counselors respond quickly to students' requests through the Web site and allow students to set the pace during their online counseling sessions. The Web page that launches the Cyber Counseling Net uses language students understand and assures them of a private conversation in the private chat room of the Palace, the site for real time conversation on Net-TLC+:

> Wanna talk? Need someone who will listen too . . . and maybe even help?
> If you've got something on your mind and could use some help, but don't know where to turn without feeling embarrassed, uncomfortable or confused, Student Counseling Net may be just what you are looking for! We are sincere, caring school counselors who are just a point and click away. You may not be able to see us, but we will surely listen and respond to your needs quickly no matter what they are. (Net-TLC+ 2001)

Students are invited to contact Cyber Counseling Net by e-mail to schedule a time for them to talk with a counselor through the Internet site:

> To set up a conversation with one of our counselors, e-mail us from anywhere, with a couple of dates and times that work for you (or let us know if it is urgent) and address your request to our coordinator at: counselor@net-tlc.org. Someone will get right back to you with a reply as soon as possible, including a scheduled time to get connected with your counselor in The Palace (the private chat room), along with easy instructions how. We look forward to hearing from you!(Net-TLC+ 2001)

The Cyber Counseling Net also provides links in both English and Spanish to educational Web sites of interest to students.

The Community Network (C-Net), was designed to involve parents and community members more fully in the schools in the Centennial BOCES. The C-Net provides information about member school districts and schools, the opportunity to communicate with parent liaisons in the schools, and news about community and school resources and events. C-Net also includes a calendar of events and activities of interest to parents, including workshops on parenting skills, opportunities for adult literacy classes, and school events. It provides links to local libraries, vocational education, and ESL classes for adults. There is space on C-Net for parents to engage in threaded conversations and for a directory of community resources. Information about the MEES program is posted on the C-Net, as well as information for parents involved in the MEES program. The Net-TLC+ project provides training for parents on the use of the Web site to ensure that they have access to C-Net.

The MEES site directory includes links to sites that provide information about prenatal development and early childhood development, information for migrant families, and information on literacy and ESL. It also offers opportunities to access the MEES Web site in Spanish and to suggest other links to add to the site.

The Administrator Net (A-Net), assists administrators to support teachers in their schools and school districts so that they can help students meet challenging content and performance standards. The A-Net connects administrators across school districts and with their own cyber mentors. The A-Net includes an interactive calendar of events and activities; legal updates; a directory of Net-TLC+ participants and resource partners; hotlinks to e-mail addresses and Web sites; an online bulletin board and chat room for threaded discussions; and a Palace chat room for professional development and individual or small group consultations.

One link on the A-Net connects administrators with the Colorado Department of Education Web site; other links lead to such sites as the Colorado Department of Education Standards Web site, the U.S. Department of Education, and the Federal Register. The searchable directory of participants and resource partners allows administrators to search by name, by biography, or by project date to communicate with any of the participants or partners. Searching on the name of Margaret Walpole, the director of compensatory education for the Centennial BOCES, for example, provides a link to her e-mail address and an extensive biography.

To support administrators in using technology in general, and A-Net in particular, the Centennial BOCES has provided one-on-one technical support and professional development. This support, in addition to the cyber mentors available through the project, is offered to help administrators to be prepared to support their teachers' use of technology in instructional and assessment activities in their classrooms. To provide additional opportunities for school superintendents to communicate and collaborate, to solve problems collectively, and to identify resources available to the school districts, the Net-TLC+ project is currently piloting videoconferencing technology.

An additional component of the Net-TLC+ project is the selection and training of a cadre of high school student apprentices. This component of the project is intended to develop at each high school a network of students who can serve as technology mentors and troubleshooters for their peers and for teachers in their schools. These high school students participate in training provided by Dream Team Technologies, the business partner of the Centennial BOCES in the Net-TLC+ project and the designer of the Net-TLC+ Web site. Through this project component, "students increase their skills in the use of technology for problem solving and learning, serve as technology mentors and troubleshooters in their respective schools, and provide effective peer training on curriculum-based educational software" (Centennial BOCES Net-TLC+ Project Brochure, n.d.).

Web TV

In 2001, the Centennial BOCES began a Web TV project to provide Internet access to migrant families in their homes. The Web TV project, funded through Title I Migrant Education Program funds and the Centennial BOCES, addresses the Colorado "state content standards in reading and writing with a focus on language arts and ESL along with dropout prevention through counseling and resource linking" (Centennial BOCES 2001b, 10).

When it is fully implemented, the Web TV project will place Web TV units in the homes of fifty migrant families. The project will also supply Internet-provider service in the homes of Web TV families if they do not already have it. A Web TV unit connects the telephone and television with a keyboard to access the Internet at a cost much lower than that required for access through a computer. The Centennial BOCES notes in a description of the Web TV project that "the use of this innovative medium allows migratory children and their families in rural and remote districts to have access to the full range of curriculum that matches district standards" (Centennial BOCES 2001b, 1).

Migrant families are selected to participate in the Web TV project based on their interest, their motivation, and their need to access the Internet. Once selected, families are trained in the use of the Web TV in a series of five training sessions; each family is assigned a bilingual or ESL teacher who participates in the training as an equal partner, and who continues to serve as the family's Web TV coach to "guide the way by blending 'high tech' with 'high touch' in a coordinated and efficient manner" (Centennial BOCES 2001b, 1).

In addition to the five training sessions, families in the Web TV project receive ongoing assistance and support from their teacher coaches to "expand communication and learning" between and among migrant families and teachers. A project listserve has been developed to facilitate daily e-mail contact among the fifty families, their teacher coaches, and other Web TV project staff members. Families and their teacher coaches also participate in further training to help the families access all the benefits available through this Internet connection as well as assistance from school counselors on education-related issues such as secondary and postsecondary education and career planning.

Margaret Walpole notes that Web TV has the potential to break down many of the barriers faced by migrant families as they seek to access education for themselves and their children:

> As part of the Web TV project, families will discover sites that help their children do their homework, making the homework more fun and exciting. They will be able to explore the world guided by their interest, help their children communicate with other countries, including Mexico and the rest of the Latin world. The Web will help their family expand their knowledge in both English and Spanish and other languages if they choose. They will have the opportunity to become citizens, not only of this country, but of the world as well. (Centennial BOCES 2001b, 3)

Web TV also holds the promise of involving parents more fully in their children's education as parents learn and explore the Internet with their children and as they establish relationships as equals with teachers.

Students, parents, and teachers in the first group of Web TV trainees all responded enthusiastically to their adventures with Web TV, according to Margaret Walpole. Ms. Walpole shared some of the messages the Centennial BOCES received from these participants via the Internet once they were connected at home.

One student wrote, "Thank you for the class of the Web TV. I really enjoyed what you did for me. Gracias. Con mucho cariño."

Another student, excited about the Web sites he had learned about during the training, wrote to thank the Web TV parent trainer, Paul Hume.

> Hey Pablo. I got the message and the Yupi site. I checked it out and it worked good. This site has everything that is needed. I can look at sports and other things that interest me. Also the things are very easy to find even my mom could do it. Thanks for the site it will be very useful.

Parents and children were encouraged to use the language they felt most comfortable with in the training. Some of them responded in English, others in Spanish. According to Paul Hume,

> The following note reflects the joy as a result of experiencing a small miracle during one of the training sessions. Even though this family

comes from a small town in Chihuahua, Mexico, we were still able to find an article about their "pueblo" on the Internet and everyone was captivated by the experience. They also mention how much it helps their children with their homework.

These parents wrote,

> Estamos muy agradecidos de haber estado en el programa especial-mente por que estamos aprendiendo muchas cosas hasta hemos po-dido ir a nuesto pueblo cosa que you ni en el pensamiento tenia. Y mas para mis hijos ya que les ayudara en sus tareas.
> *We are very grateful to have been in the program especially because we are learning many things. We've even been able to go back to our town [via the Internet], something we've never imagined. Even more so for our children because it helps them with their homework.* (Centennial BOCES 2001b, 7)

One of the teachers who participated in the project worked with several of the families at their homes, helping them to connect their Web TV devices and to get online. She reported the following:

> Yay!!! We set the "famruiz" online, *rojo por rojo, blanco por blanco* etc., and you should see the resolution on the big-screen TV!!!!!. Again, we went to Yupi.com, and the family gathered and quietly, but excitedly, asked Gabriela to click on different topics of interest. . . . . soccer, weather, news. A great moment came when I gently put the keyboard in the papa's hands, who was very leery of it at first! With Gabriela showing him how, I left an hour and a half later, . . . with dad and daughter playing checkers on line! E-mail was a big hit, too, and they will be calling relatives in Wisconsin and Mexico to get their addresses!!! As I typed in the initial letter, it was they who became *los maestros*, and "caught" some typing errors I inevitably make on e-mail! I know that famgalvan is online, too! I can't wait to meet with them and feel the excitement of four teenage daughters getting a phone, never mind Internet/e-mail access! Esmeralda is thrilled when she comes to class and talks about these new adventures. (Centennial BOCES 2001b, 12)

This teacher noted that she was truly an equal partner with the families in this project. "The beautiful thing about this is that I am *la estudiente y maestra,* and my families are very appreciate of my efforts. I've no-ticed that they are taking more risks in writing English to me since I've started doing likewise in *Español!!.* . . . Our comfort level with each other and with the technology has greatly increased!" (Centennial BOCES 2001b, 11).

Although the Web TV project has just begun in the spring of 2001, it has the potential for a number of positive outcomes, all important to the educational success of migrant children and their parents. One of the most important benefits of the Web TV project is the access these migrant children and their families have to technology and the Internet; such access ensures the equity of resources called for by Standard 1 of the National Association of State Directors of Migrant Education Opportunity to Learn Standards. Using the Internet on a regular basis will increase the amount of time these children spend interacting with English text, one of the most important factors in developing proficiency in the English language arts. The Web TV also has the potential to develop family literacy, to strengthen the relationship between migrant parents and teachers and other school personnel, and to increase parental involvement in the school.

The Net-TLC+ project, together with the Web TV project, meets all of the criteria DiCerbo (2001) identified as part of effective instructional programs for migrant children. Both projects focus on respect for diversity. Much of the professional development provided through the Net-TLC+ project is focused on developing effective instructional practices for English-language learners through sheltered English; the Web TV training that builds personal connections between teachers and families provides opportunities for teachers and families to learn about each other's cultures, experiences, and values. The Internet also opens doors for children and families to know and experience the world.

Both Net-TLC+ and the Web TV project honor students' and their families' culture and language by providing the opportunity for them to work, as well as access information, in both Spanish and English. Many of the schools in the Centennial BOCES are dual-language schools that allow students to learn content in their first language while they develop literacy in English.

Including children in the training for the Web TV project and training high school students to be apprentices show that students are valued; further, students have the opportunities described by DiCerbo to demonstrate initiative, competence, and responsibility. These experiences contribute to the enhancement of the children's self-concept and self-esteem that is so critical if they are to be successful in school.

In addition to their experience with using the Internet, the learning opportunities provided students as a result of the professional development their teachers participate in through Net-TLC+ help students develop the metacognitive skills necessary for them to become independent learners. Through the Net-TLC+ project, teachers have learned and continue to learn about effective standards-based instruction and assessment, helping them to make appropriate decisions about children's learning. Involving migrant parents as partners in their children's education, as Web TV has the potential to do, can also contribute to making better decisions about children's appropriate placement in educational programs.

Administrators in the Centennial BOCES have been involved in professional development to develop a better understanding of the needs of second-language learners and effective strategies for second-language teaching; this allows them to be instructional leaders who do make migrant children a priority in their schools. They have also developed a teacher evaluation instrument that allows them to document teachers' effectiveness in meeting the needs of English-language learners.

Through the Net-TLC+ and the Web TV projects, Centennial BOCES has demonstrated its commitment to leveling the playing field for the migrant students served by the school districts of the BOCES. In the words of one Centennial BOCES staff member, "I think the rewards will be deeper and last longer than we can imagine" (Centennial BOCES 2001b, 11).

REFERENCES

Board of Cooperative Education Services (Centennial BOCES). *Compensatory Education*. Greeley, CO: Board of Cooperative Education Services, n.d.

——. *Networks in Technology as Learning Communities* (Net-TLC+). Project Brochure. Greeley, CO: Board of Cooperative Education Services, n.d.

——. Compensatory Education Program. *Networks in Technology as Learning Communities: Success Stories*. Greeley, CO: Board of Cooperative Education Services, 2001a.

——. *Web TV Project*. Greeley, CO: Board of Cooperative Education Services, 2001b.

DiCerbo, P. "Why Migrant Education Matters." *Issue & Brief No. 8*. Washington, DC: National Clearinghouse for Bilingual Education Center for the Study of Language & Education, 2001. Available: http://www/ncbe.gwu.edu

Dream Team Technologies. "Case Study: Net-TLC+: Technology Connecting Teachers and Students to Key Resources." Denver, CO: Dream Team Technologies, 1999.

Networks in Technology as Learning Communities (Net-TLC+). 2001. Available: http://www.NET-TLC.org

Chapter Seven

☛ Directory of Organizations, Associations, and Government Agencies

The organizations, associations, and agencies listed here are all involved in administering migrant education programs, providing technical assistance to migrant education programs, assisting migrant children, youth, and adults access appropriate education programs, or advocating for educational, health care, and other opportunities for migrant children, youth, and adults.

GOVERNMENT AGENCIES

National Center for ESL Literacy Education (NCLE)
4646 40th Street, NW
Washington, DC 20016-1859
(202) 263-0700, ext. 200
www.cal.org/ncle

The National Center for ESL Literacy Education (NCLE) is a national information center that focuses on the language and literacy education of adults and out-of-school youth learning English. NCLE collaborates with the U.S. Department of Education, Office of Vocational and Adult Education; the National Institute for Literacy; the National Center for the Study of Adult Learning and Literacy; Teachers of English to Speakers of Other Languages (TESOL); the Office of Refugee Resettlement; Delta Systems, Inc.; the Andrew W. Mellon Foundation Project in Adult Immigrant Education; the Lexicon School of Languages, Inc.; and City Family Publishers to provide information on adult ESL literacy to teachers, tutors, program directors, researchers, and policymakers interested in the education of refugees, immigrants, and other U.S. residents whose native language is other than English. The NCLE Web site provides information about adult ESL, as well as links to several of its collaborating agencies.

Office of Bilingual Education and Minority Languages Affairs (OBEMLA)
400 Maryland Avenue SW
Washington, DC 20202-6510
Contact: Art Love, Acting Director
www.ed.gov/offices/OBEMLA

The Office of Bilingual Education and Minority Languages Affairs (OBLEMA) was established in 1974 to help school districts meet their responsibility of providing equal educational opportunities to children with limited English proficiency. The group's mission is to ensure equal access to education and to promote educational excellence through the nation.

Office of Migrant Education
U.S. Department of Education/OESE
600 Independence Avenue SW
Room 4100, Portals Building
Washington, DC 20202-6135
(202) 260-1164
Contac: Francisco Garcia, Director
www.ed.gov/offices/OESE/MEP

The purpose of the Office of Migrant Education (OME) is to improve teaching and learning for migratory children. OME administers programs and projects that assist federal, state, and local agencies coordinate and provide services that will help migrant children overcome cultural and language barriers, health-related problems, and other challenges that place these children at risk of not completing their education.

STATE AGENCIES

Each state has its own office of migrant education whose charge it is to administer federally funded migrant education programs in the state. These offices oversee (and in some states conduct) identification and recruitment efforts, provide professional development and other technical assistance, and gather data about the effectiveness of the programs.

Alabama

Alabama Department of Education
Federal Programs
5348 Gordon Persons Building

Montgomery, AL 36130
Contact: Hannis Roberts, Education Specialist
Phone: (334) 242-8199   Fax: (334) 242-0496

Alaska

Alaska Department of Education
801 West 10th Street Suite 200
Juneau, AK 99801
Contact: Carole Green, Program Manager Migrant Education
Phone: (907) 465-2886   Fax: (907) 465-2989
carole_green@educ.state.ak.us
http://www.eed.state.ak.us

Arizona

Academic Support Division
1535 West Jefferson 1st Floor
Phoenix, AZ 85007
Contact: Ralph Romero, Director
Phone: (602) 542-7462   Fax: (602) 542-3100
rromero@mail1.ade.state.az.us
http://www.ade.state.az.us

Arkansas

Arkansas Migrant Education Program
501 Woodlane Suite 226
Little Rock, AR 72201
Contact: William Cosme, Director
Phone: (501) 324-9660   Fax: (501) 324-9694
miged@loki.k12.ar.us

California

Migrant Education Program
721 Capitol Mall
P.O. Box 944272
Sacramento, CA 94244
Contact: Larry Jaurequi, Migrant Education State Director
Phone: (916) 657-2561   Fax: (916) 657-2869

Colorado

Colorado Department of Education
201 E. Colfax Avenue Room 401
Denver, CO 80201
Contact: Prax Martinez, Director
Phone: (303) 866-6870   Fax: (303) 866-6857
martinez_p@cde.state.co.us

Connecticut

Connecticut Department of Migrant Education
P.O. Box 2219
Hartford, CT 06145
Contact: Marlene Padernacht, Migrant Education State Director
Phone: (860) 566-3278   Fax: (860) 566-7845
Marlene.padernacht@po.state.ct.us

Delaware

Migrant Education State Director
Delaware Department of Education
Townsend Building
P.O. Box 1402
Dover, DE 19903
Contact: Sister Margaret Loveland, Education Specialist
Phone: (302) 739-2770   Fax: (302) 739-4483
mloveland@state.de.us

Florida

Migrant Education State Director
Florida Department of Education
Turlington Building Room 306
Tallahassee, FL 32399
Contact: William Pittman, Jr., Administrator
Phone: (850) 487-3530   Fax: (850) 922-9648

Georgia

Georgia Department of Education Migrant/ESOL Programs
Twin Towers East Suite 1852
205 Butler Street SE

Atlanta, GA 30334
Contact: Peggy Kent
Phone: (404) 656-4995   Fax: (404) 651-8079
pkent@doe.k12.ga.us
http://www.doe.k12.ga.us

Hawaii

Hawaii District Office
76 Aupuni Street
P.O. Box 4160
Hilo, HI 96720
Contact: Patricia C. Bergin, District Superintendent
Phone: (808) 327-4991   Fax: (808) 974-6604

Idaho

Idaho Department of Education
650 West State Street
P.O. Box 83720
Boise, ID 83720
Contact: Irene Chavolla, Coordinator
Phone: (208) 332-6907   Fax: (208) 334-2636
ichavoll@sde.state.id.us

Illinois

Illinois State Board of Education
100 North First Street E-233
Springfield, IL 62777
Contact: David Gutierrez, Principal Education Consultant
Phone: (217) 782-5728   Fax: (217) 524-9354

Indiana

Migrant Education Program
State House Room 229
Indianapolis, IN 46204
Contact: Darlene Slaby, Migrant Education State Director
Phone: (317) 232-0555   Fax: (317) 236-9571

Iowa

Migrant Education Program
Iowa Department of Education
Grimes State Office Building
Des Moines, IA 50319
Contact: Donna Eggleston, Migrant Education Director/Consultant
Phone: (515) 281-7844   Fax: (515) 242-6019
donna.eggleston@ed.state.ia.us

Kansas

Migrant Education Program
120 SE 10th Avenue
Topeka, KS 66612
Contact: Ron Johnson, Migrant Education State Director
Phone: (785) 296-2600   Fax: (785) 296-5867
rjohn@smtpgw.ksbe.state.ks.us

Kentucky

Migrant Education Program
Kentucky Department of Education
Capitol Plaza Tower
500 Mero Street Suite 830
Frankfort, KY 40601
Contact: Ken Ison, Migrant Coordinator
Phone: (502) 564-3791   Fax: (502) 564-8149
kison@kde.state.ky.us
www.kde.state.ky.us/osis/resources/comp/migrant/default.asp

Louisiana

Bureau of Migrant Education
654 Main Street
P.O. Box 94064
Baton Rouge, LA 70804
Contact: Ronnie Glover, Director
Phone: (504) 342-3517   Fax: (504) 342-6485
jgrant@mail.doe.state.la.us

Maine

Migrant Education State Director
Maine Department of Education
State House Station #19
Augusta, ME 04333
Contact: Pam Gatcomb, Coordinator
Phone: (207) 287-5174　Fax: (207) 287-5306
pam.gatcomb@state.me.us

Maryland

Migrant Education Program
700 Glasgow Street
P.O. Box 619
Cambridge, MD 21613
Contact: Cvieta Sheridan, Migrant Education State Director
Phone: (410) 221-0151　Fax: (410) 221-1085
mesc@dmv.com

Massachusetts

Migrant Education Program
20 Kent Street
Brookline, MA 02146
Contact: Miriam Schwartz, Migrant Education State Director
Phone: (617) 738-5600　Fax: (617) 738-0968
schwarm@meol.mass.edu

Michigan

Migrant Education State Director
Michigan Department of Education
Office of Field Services
608 West Allegan
P.O. Box 30008
Lansing, MI 48909
Contact: Linda Brown, Supervisor Central Support Unit
Phone: (517) 373-3921　Fax: (517) 335-2886
brownlq@state.mi.us

Minnesota

Migrant Education State Director
Minnesota Department of Children Families and Learning
1500 Highway 36 West
Roseville, MN 55113
Contact: Mary Pfeifer, Supervisor
Phone: (651) 582-8700

Mississippi

Migrant Education State Director
Mississippi Department of Education
359 North West Street Suite 162
P.O. Box 771
Jackson, MS 39205
Contact: Rita Lane, Supervisor
Phone: (601) 359-3499   Fax: (601) 359-2587

Missouri

Migrant Education State Director
Federal Grants Management
205 Jefferson Street
P.O. Box 480
Jefferson City, MO 65102
Contact: Shawn Cockrum, Supervisor
Phone: (573) 751-2046   Fax: (573) 526-6698

Montana

Title 1/Migrant Program
P.O. Box 202501
Helena, MT 59620
Contact: Angela Branz-Spall, Director
Phone: (406) 444-2423   Fax: (406) 449-7105
angelab@opi.mt.gov

Nebraska

Migrant Education State Director
Nebraska Department of Education
301 Centennial Mall South

P.O. Box 94987
Lincoln, NE 68509
Contact: Dr. Elizabeth Alfred, Director
Phone: (402) 471-3440   Fax: (402) 471-2701

Nevada

Migrant Education Program
700 East 5th Street
Carson City, NV 89701
Contact: Gary Pierson, Migrant Education State Director
Phone: (702) 687-9161   Fax: (702) 687-9123

New Hampshire

Migrant Education Program
101 Pleasant Street
Concord, NH 03301
Contact: Rose Savino, Migrant Education State Director
Phone: (603) 271-2273   Fax: (603) 271-1953

New Jersey

Migrant Education Program
New Jersey Department of Education
Route 29 Riverview Plaza
Building 100 2nd Floor CN 500
Trenton, NJ 08625
Contact: Anne Corwell, Program Specialist
Phone: (609) 633-1304   Fax: (609) 633-6874

New Mexico

Migrant Education Program
New Mexico Department of Education
300 Don Gasper Street
Santa Fe, NM 87501
Contact: Bobby Gomez, Migrant Director
Phone: (505) 827-6527   Fax: (505) 827-6504
bgomez@sde.state.nm.us

New York

Migrant Education Program
New York Education Department
Room 483 EBA
Albany, NY 12234
Contact: Nancy Croce, Director
Phone: (518) 474-9392   Fax: (518) 473-1714

North Carolina

Migrant Education Program
North Carolina Department of Public Instruction
301 North Wilmington Street
Raleigh, NC 27601
Contact: Rachel Crawford, Migrant Consultant
Phone: (919) 715-1828   Fax: (919) 715-1897

North Dakota

Migrant Education Program
600 East Boulevard
Bismarck, ND 58505
Contact: Sandy Aune, Migrant Education State Director
Phone: (701) 328-2170   Fax: (701) 328-4770}

Ohio

Migrant Education Program
Federal Assistance Division
933 High Street
Worthington, OH 43085
Contact: Dr. Jose Villa, Director
Phone: (614) 466-4161   Fax: (614) 751-1622

Oklahoma

Migrant Education Program
Oklahoma Department of Education
2500 North Lincoln Suite I-33
Oklahoma City, OK 73105
Contact: Frank Rexach, Title I/MEP Director
Phone: (405) 521-2893   Fax: (405) 521-2998

Oregon

Migrant Education Program
Oregon Department of Education
255 Capitol Street NE
Salem, OR 97310
Contact: Ernestina (Tina) L. Garcia
Phone: (503) 378-3606 ext. 675   Fax: (503) 373-7968
Tina.garcia@state.or.us

Pennsylvania

Migrant Education Program
333 Market Street 5th Floor
Harrisburg, PA 17126
Contact: Dr. Manuel Recio, Migrant Education State Director
Phone: (717) 783-6464   Fax: (717) 783-4392
pameo@epix.net

Puerto Rico

Puerto Rico Migrant Education Program
P.O. Box 190759
San Juan, PR 00919
Contact: Maria T. Fret Mercado, Director
Phone: (787) 759-8910 ext. 283   Fax: (787) 751-3798

Rhode Island

Migrant Education Program
Rhode Island Department of Education
255 Westminster Street
Providence, RI 02903
Contact: Susan Rotblat-Walker, MEP Spec.
Phone: (401) 222-2651   Fax: (401) 222-2734

South Carolina

Migrant Education Program
South Carolina Department of Education
1429 Senate Street Room 503
Columbia, SC 29201
Contact: Jess Torres, Director

Phone: (803) 734-8111   Fax: (803) 734-4605
jtorres@sde.state.sc.us

South Dakota

Migrant Education Program
700 Governor's Drive
Pierre, SD 57501
Contact: Janet Ricketts, Migrant Education State Director
Phone: (605) 773-3218   Fax: (605) 773-3782

Tennessee

Migrant Education Program
Tennessee Department of Education
8th Floor Gateway Plaza
710 James Robinson Parkway
Nashville, TN 37243
Contact: Roberta Bobbie Jackson, Director
Phone: (615) 532-6297   Fax: (615) 532-8536
rjackson@mail.state.tn.us

Texas

Migrant Education Program
1701 North Congress Avenue
Austin, TX 78701
Contact: Frank Contreras, Migrant Education State Director
Phone: (512) 463-9067   Fax: (512) 463-9759
shuerta@mail4.tea.texas.gov

Utah

Migrant Education Program
Services for Students At Risk
250 East 500 South
Salt Lake City, UT 84111
Contact: David Gomez
Phone: (801) 538-7725
dgomez@usoe.k12.ut.us

Vermont

Vermont Migrant Education Program
120 State Street
Montpelier, VT 05620
Contact: Mary Mulloy
Phone: (800) 639-2023   Fax: (802) 828-3146
mmulloy@doe.state.vt.us

Virginia

Title I/Migrant Education
P.O. Box 2120
Richmond, VA 23218
Contact: Denise Perritt, Education Specialist
Phone: (804) 371-7579   Fax: (804) 371-7347

Washington

Migrant Education Program
Instructional Support Services
Old Capitol Building
P.O. Box 47200
Olympia, WA 98504
Contact: Raul de la Rosa, Director
Phone: (360) 753-1137   Fax: (360) 664-2605

West Virginia

Migrant Education Program
1900 Kanawha Blvd. East
Building 6 Room B330
Charleston, WV 25305
Contact: Suzette Cook, Migrant Education State Director
Phone: (304) 558-7805   Fax: (304) 558-0459

Wisconsin

Migrant Education Program
Special Needs Section
Wisconsin Department of Public Instruction
125 South Webster Street
P.O. Box 7841

Madison, WI 53707
Contact: Dr. Myrna Toney
Phone: (608) 266-9629   Fax: (608) 267-0364
Toneymm@mail.state.wi.us

Wyoming

Migrant Education Program
Wyoming Department of Education
Hathaway Building 2nd Floor
1200 Capitol Avenue
Cheyenne, WY 82002
Contact: Kaye McCrary, Migrant Director
Phone: (307) 777-7633   Fax: (307) 777-6234

OTHER STATE AGENCIES

Texas Migrant Interstate Program
P.O. Drawer Y
Pharr, TX 78577
Contact: Tomas Yánez
Phone: (800) 292-7006   Fax: (956) 702-6058
tyanez@hiline.net
http://www.hiline.net/~psjaisd/migrant/tmip.html

The Texas Migrant Interstate Program (TMIP) was established in 1981 to improve the high school graduation rate of migrant students by facilitating the intrastate and interstate coordination efforts of the Migrant Education Program. TMIP assists with the exchange of credit accrual information between students' home-base and receiving schools, provides technical assistance and professional development in secondary credit accrual and in improving the graduation rate for teachers and other educational personnel, and promotes coordination and collaboration between migrant educational programs.

OTHER AGENCIES AND ORGANIZATIONS

Academy for Educational Development
Migrant Head Start Quality Improvement Center
1825 Connecticut Avenue NW
Washington, DC 20009
Contact: Leilani Pennel, Project Director

(800) 864-0465
mhsqic.org

The Quality Improvement Center provides training and technical assistance aimed at improving the quality of Migrant Head Start programs.

Binational Program
California/Mexico Visiting Teacher
Ventura County
Superintendent of Schools Office
5189 Verdugo Way
Camarillo, CA 93012
Contact: Gil Villaseñor, Coordinator
(805) 383-1924 or (800) 451-9697
region7.cu.edu/binational/

This organization promotes and facilitates collaboration and communication, including conference and teacher exchanges, between education programs in the United States and Mexico. The Binational Program has also developed a Binational Transfer Document to facilitate exchange of student records.

Catholic Migrant Farmworker Network
1915 University Drive
Boise, ID 83706
Contact: Celine Caufield
(208) 384-1778
www.cmfn.org

In addition to pastoral services, this organization provides information about migrant issues such as housing and health care, and political action and advocacy for migrant farmworkers and their families.

ESCORT (Eastern Stream Center on Resources and Training)
State University of New York at Oneonta
305 Bugbee Hall
Oneonta, NY 13820
Contact: Bob Levy
(800) 234-8848 (migrant hotline)
(800) 451-8058
www.oneonta.edu/~thomasr./800.html

The hotline is a twenty-four-hour service available to migrant families nationwide. The hotline helps families find local migrant education programs and other needed services in communities across the country.

Illinois Migrant Council
28 East Jackson Blvd., 16th Floor
Chicago, IL 60604
(312) 663-1522
www.illinoismigrant.org
Contact: Eloy Salazar, Executive Director, Brenda Pessin,
Director, Education

The Illinois Migrant Council is a community-based nonprofit organization. Its primary mission is to promote employment, educational, and other opportunities for migrant and seasonal farmworkers and their families. The Illinois Migrant Council, which was organized in 1966, is currently involved various migrant education projects, including ★Estrella, a distance learning education project, and a migrant Even Start project.

Interhemispheric Resource Center
www.irc-online.org

The Interhemispheric Resource Center (IRC) is an organization whose mission is to make the United States a more responsible global leader and partner. The IRC publishes an online journal, *borderlines,* in English and Spanish. The journal explores and discusses binational and global social, political, educational, and environmental issues. The IRC also supports a project called BIOS, Border Information & Outreach Service.

Interstate Migrant Education Council
One Massachusetts Avenue, NW
Suite 700
Washington, DC 20001
Contact: John D. Perry, Nancy Clark Wiehe
(202) 336-7078
www.migedimec.org

The Interstate Migrant Education Council facilitates interstate sharing of information about model migrant education programs and works to develop interventions that address the educational consequences of such issues as student mobility, intermittent attendance, and limited English proficiency.

Mexican American Legal Defense and Educational Fund
National Headquarters
634 South Spring Street
11th Floor

Los Angeles, CA 90014
(213) 629-2512
www.MALDEF.org

The Mexican American Legal Defense and Educational Fund (MALDEF) exists to protect and promote the civil rights of Latinos living in the United States. MALDEF uses litigation, advocacy, community education, and collaboration to secure rights in the areas of employment, education, immigration, political access, and language.

Migrant Clinicians Network
Contact: Karen Mountain, RN, MSN, MBA, Executive Director
kmountain@migrantclinician.org
www. cmfn.org
www.migrantclinician.org

This network of clinicians across the United States and Puerto Rico conducts research on migrant health issues, develops public health information and materials for use with migrant farmworkers, and provides national and binational patient tracking and referrals for patients with tuberculosis and diabetes. The Migrant Clinicians Network also seeks to promote the health of farmworkers by acting as a national and international voice on migrant health issues through leadership, advocacy, and partnership with collaborating agencies.

Migrant Head Start
Administration for Children and Families/Head Start Bureau
Box 1182
Washington, DC 20013
Contact: Maria T. Candamil
(202) 205-8572

The Administration for Children and Families provides Head Start services for children of eligible migrant farmworkers across the country and offers technical assistance to Migrant Head Start grantees and delegate agencies.

Migrant Health Program
www.bphc.hrsa.dhhs.gov/mhc/mhc1.htm

The Migrant Health Centers (MHC) provide migrant and seasonal farmworkers and their families access to comprehensive medical care services that have a culturally sensitive focus.

**Migration and Refugee Services/Pastoral Care
of Migrants and Refugees**
U.S. Catholic Conference
3211 4th Street NE
Washington, DC 20017
Contact: Mark Franken, Executive Director
(202) 541-3035
www.ncc.buscc.org

This organization addresses how the Catholic Church should respond to issues related to migrants and refugees. The organization also provides advocacy and pastoral care directly to migrant and seasonal farmworkers.

National Association for Bilingual Education (NABE)
1220 L Street NW
Suite 605
Washington, DC 20005
(202) 898-1829
www.nabe.org

The National Association for Bilingual Education (NABE) is a membership organization devoted to representing the interests of language-minority students, bilingual education teachers, and parents of language minority students. The organization publishes a journal, *NABE News* that publishes information about bilingual education and second-language acquisition, as well as the *Bilingual Research Journal.* NABE sponsors an annual conference for bilingual educators.

**National Association of State Directors of
Migrant Education (NASDME)**
11768 S. Harrel's Ferry Road, Suite F
Baton Rouge, LA 70816
Contact: Dr. Myrna Toney, President
www.nasdme.org
nasdme@bellsouth.net

The National Association of State Directors of Migrant Education (NASDME) serves as a vehicle for dialogue among state directors of migrant education and supports collaborative efforts among its members. NASDME advocates on behalf of migrant children and migrant education prograIt also sponsors an annual migrant education conference.

National Center for Farmworker Health

www.ncfh.org/aboutncfh/aboutncfh.htm

A multifaceted organization that provides a wide range of services and information related to farmworker health issues. The organization is dedicated to improving the health of the workers who harvest crops in the United States. The National Center's Web site provides detailed descriptions of the services and information available from the organization.

National Center for Farmworker Health, Inc.

P.O. Box 150009
Austin, TX 78715
(512) 312-2700, (800) 377-9968
www.ncfh.org

The National Center for Farmworker Health, Inc., is a private, nonprofit organization that provides services to improve the health of migrant farmworkers. The center coordinates various projects related to migrant health, including educating the larger public about the health care issues of migrant farmworkers, developing and disseminating materials for use with migrant farmworkers by health care professionals, researching migrant health issues, brokering resources for migrant farmworkers and their families, and improving access to health care for migrant farmworkers and their families in the Central Stream.

Call for Health, one of the National Center's projects, offers a referral service for farmworkers via a toll-free telephone number. The telephone line is answered by workers who can provide information in English and Spanish to farmworkers, as well as health care providers. The hotline also provides translation services and service coordination for farmworkers in the Central Stream.

Another of the National Center's projects, the Traveling Lay Health Advisor Project, is sponsored by the Division of Cancer Prevention and Control of the National Center for Chronic Disease Prevention and Promotion that is part of the Center for Disease Control and Prevention. The project involves the provision of referrals to health care services through trained lay health advisors from Laredo, El Paso, and Eagle Pass, Texas, who travel the migrant stream. This project is aimed at providing education to Latina farmworker women on the detection and treatment of breast and cervical cancer. The project is active in Arizona, Colorado, Illinois, Indiana, Iowa, Kansas, Michigan, Minnesota, Missouri, Montana, Nebraska, New Mexico, Ohio, Texas, and Wisconsin.

National Council of La Raza
1111 19th Street NW
Suite 1000
Washington, DC 20036
Contact: Marcela Urrupla, Policy Analyst
(800) 311-NCLR
www.nclr.org

The National Council of La Raza (NCLR) provides advocacy in problems of discrimination and poverty for Hispanics, both directly and through over 200 affiliate organizations in thirty-seven states, Puerto Rico, and the District of Columbia.

National Parent Center
National Coalition of Title I/Chapter 1 Parents
1541 14th Street NW
Washington, DC 20005
Contact: Bob Witherspoon, Executive Director
(202) 547-9286

The National Parent Center provides information on how parents can be involved in their children's education in general, and more specifically, Title I prograThe National Parent Center is also an advocacy organization for parents whose children participate in Title I programs.

National PASS Center
Geneseo Migrant Center
27 Lackawanna Avenue
Mt. Morris, NY 14510
(716) 668-7960, (800) 245-5681
pass@migrant.net

This center provides leadership for the Portable Assisted Study Sequence (PASS), serving as a clearinghouse and overseeing course development and revision. General information about PASS, as well as information about specific courses and their administration, is available from the National PASS Center.

Quality Education for Minorities Network
1818 N. Street NW
Suite 3350
Washington, DC 20036
(202) 659-1818
http://qemnetwork.qem.org

The Quality Education for Minorities (QEM) Network is a nonprofit organization dedicated to improving the education of African Americans, Alaska Natives, American Indians, Mexican Americans, and Puerto Ricans. The QEM Network provides advocacy, community outreach, professional development for educators, and information about such programs as mathematics, science, and engineering initiatives aimed at minority students. The organization also maintains an electronic bulletin board of public policy and legislation related to its mission.

MEXICAN INSTITUTES AND CULTURAL CENTERS

The twenty-one Mexican Institutes and Cultural Centers in the United States provide information about Mexican culture and educational materials to help Mexican citizens and Mexican Americans in the United States connect to their rich heritage. The institutes and centers sponsor teacher exchanges between teachers in the United States and Mexico and other educational prograThey also assist parents and schools with Binational Transfer Documents.

Agrupación de Comunidades Mexicanes
380 North First Street, Suite 102
San Jose, CA 95112
(408) 294-3415

Centro Cultural Mexicano
1200 N.W. 78th Avenue, Suite 200
Miami, FL 33126
(305) 716-4977

111 South Independence
East Mall
Bourse Bldg., Suite 1010
Philadelphia, PA 19106
(215) 625-4897

Centro Mexicano de Atlanta
3220 Peachtree Road N.E.
Atlanta, GA 30305
(404) 264-1240

Centro Mexicano de Denver
48 Steele Street
Denver, CO 80206
(303) 331-1870

Centro Mexicano de Estado de Washington
2132 Third Avenue
Seattle, WA 98121
(206) 441-0552

Centro Cultural Mexicano del Norte de California
1010 8th Street
Sacramento, CA 95814
(916) 446-3691

Centro Cultural Mexicano Paso del Norte
910 East San Antonio Street
El Paso, TX 79901
(915) 533-6311

Centro Cultural Mexicano de Phoenix
1990 W. Camelback Road, Suite 110
Phoenix, AZ 85012
(602) 271-4858

Centro Cultural Mexicano de San Francisco
870 Market Street, Suite 528
San Francisco, CA 94102
(415) 393-8003

Centro Cultural Mexicano del Sur
#2 Canal Street, Suite 840
New Orleans, LA
(505) 522-3597

Centro Cultural Mexicano de Tucson
553 S. Stone Avenue
Tucson, AZ 85701
(520) 882-5596

Centro Cultural Mexicano de Valle de Texas
1418 Beech Street
Suites 102, 104, 106
McAllen, TX 78501
(210) 686-0243

Instituto de Cultura y Educatión de Chicago
702 North Wells
Chicago, IL 60630
(312) 606-0555

Instituto Cultural Mexicano
125 East Paseo de la Plaza Suite 300
Los Angeles, CA
(213) 624-3682

2829 Sixteenth N.W.
Washington, DC 20009
(202) 728-1628

Insitituto Cultural Mexicano de Houston
30115 Richmond, Suite 100
Houston, TX 77098
(713) 524-2951

Instituto Cultural Mexicano de Nueva York
8 East 41st Street
New York, NY 10017
(212) 725-8167

Instituto Cultural Mexicano de San Antonio
600 Hemisfair Plaza
San Antonio, TX 78205
(210) 227-0123

Instituto Mexicano del Centro de California (IMECAL)
830 Van Ness Avenue
Fresno, CA 93271
(209) 445-2615

Instituto Mexicano de San Diego
1549 India Street
San Diego, CA 92101
(619) 231-8410

HIGH SCHOOL EQUIVALENCY PROGRAMS (HEP)

The High School Equivalency Program (HEP) is intended to help migrant students complete the courses necessary to earn high school diplomas or GEDs and to be prepared for postsecondary education or the workforce. HEP programs are currently operating in twelve states and in Puerto Rico.

California

California State University, Sacramento
Cross Cultural Resource Center
6000 J Street, T-JJ Room 1
Sacramento, CA 95819-6107
Contact: Dr. Joyce M. Bishop, Director
(916) 278-3708
Jimbishop@worldnet.att.net

Jobs for Progress, Inc., Fresno Co. SER
524 S. Clovis Street, Suite 1
Fresno, CA 93727
Contact: Rebecca Mendibles, Director
(559) 452-0881
SERFRESNO@pacbell.net

Colorado

University of Colorado, Boulder
BUENO Center for Multicultural Education
Campus Box 249
Boulder, CO 80309-0249
Contact: Dr. Ray Archibeque, Director
(303) 492-3358
archibeque@colorado.edu

Florida

University of South Florida
Department of Special Education
4202 Fowler Avenue
Tampa, FL 33620-8350
Contact: Dr. Ann Cranston-Gingras, Director
(813) 974-5542
cranston@tempest.coedu.usf.edu

Idaho

Boise State University
Department of Teacher Education
1910 University Drive
Boise, ID 83725
Contact: Dr. John Jensen, Director
(208) 426-4365
jjensen@boisestate.edu

Maryland

Center for Human Services
7200 Wisconsin Avenue, Suite 600
Bethesda, MD 20814
Contact: Grogan Ullah, Director
(301) 941-8452
jullah@urc.chs.com

Mississippi

Mississippi Valley State University
Office of Continuing Education
P.O. Box 7229
Itta Bena, MS 38941
Contact: Bobbie Harris, Director

New Mexico

Northern New Mexico Community College
High School Equivalency Program
El Rito, NM 87530
Contact: Annette Garcia, Director

(505) 581-4116
agar@nnm.cc.nm.us

Oregon

Chemeketa Community College
4000 Lancaster Drive NE
P.O. Box 14007
Salem. OR 97309-7070
Contact: Cheryl Falk, Director
(503) 399-5145
falc@chemek.c.or.us

University of Oregon
College of Education
1685 E. 17th Street
Eugene, OR 97403
Contact: Emilio Hernandez, Director
(541) 346-0882

Puerto Rico

InterAmerican University of Puerto Rico
San Germán Campus
P.O. Box 5100
San Germán, PR 00683-5100
Contact: Sylvia Robles, Director
(787) 892-6380
srobles@ns.inter.edu

Tennessee

University of Tennessee
College of Education
600 Henley, Suite 312
Knoxville, TN 37996
Contact: Dr. Loida C. Velazquez, Director
(423) 974-7926
lvelazq1@utk.edu

Texas

Del Mar College
Center for Business and Community Education
101 Baldwin Street
Corpus Christi, TX 78404-3897
Contact: Chris Palacios, Director
(512) 698-1781
cpalaci@camino.delmar.edu

SER-Jobs for Progress of SW Texas, Laredo
P.O. Box 440149
Laredo, TX 78041
Contact: Elrain Sanchez, Director
(956) 724-1844
efrain@border.net

Southwest Texas State University
601 University Drive
San Marcos, TX 78566-4616
Contact: Dorcas N. Garcia, Director
(512) 245-8049
dg13@swt.edu

Texas A&M University–Kingsville
Division of Special Programs
Campus Box 181
Kingsvile, TX 78363-8202
Contact: Dr. Consuelo Martineq, Director
(512) 593-8202
kamcmoo@tamuk.edu

University of Houston
College of Education
4800 Calhoun, Suite 425FH
Houston, TX 77204-5874
Contact: Kobla Osanyade, Director
(713) 743-4985
kosayand@bayou.uh.edu

University of Texas at Brownsville and Texas Southmost College
80 Fort Brown
Brownsville, TX 78520
Contact: Edwin Barrera, Director
(956) 983-7311
ebarrera@UTB1.UBT.EDU

University of Texas at El Paso
500 W. University Avenue
El Paso, TX 79968-0571
Contact: Norma Chacon-Garcia, Director
(915) 747-5587
normac@utep.edu

University of Texas Pan American, Edinburg
1201 West University Drive
Edinburg, TX 78539
Contact: Richard Trevino, Director
(210) 381-2521
rick.trev@panam.edu

Washington

Heritage College
3250 Fort Road
Toppenish, WA 98948
Contact: Norberto Espindola, Director
(509) 865-2244
espindola_b@heritage.edu

Washington State University
College of Education
Pullman, WA 99164-2101
Contact: Dr. James T. Shoemaker, Director
(509) 335-2454
shoemake@wsu.edu

Wisconsin

Milwaukee Technical College
700 West State Street, Rm M222

Milwaukee, WI 53233-1443
Contact: Arturo Martinez, Director
(414) 297-6803
martinez@milwaukee.tec.wi.us

COLLEGE ASSISTANCE MIGRANT PROGRAM (CAMP)

The College Assistance Migrant Program (CAMP) provides academic and social support and financial aid to help migrant students be successful in their first year in college. The program also assists migrant students in finding financial aid for subsequent years. CAMP sites are located in

California

California State University, Fresno
College Assistance Migrant Program
5150 N. Maple Street
Fresno, CA 93726
(559) 278-1787

California State University, Sacramento
Office of Academic Affairs
6000 J Street
Sacramento, CA 95819-6063
(916) 278-7241

Colorado

Metropolitan State College of Denver
Campus Box 28, P.O. Box 173362
Denver, CO 80217-3362
(303) 556-6231

Georgia

Abraham Baldwin Agricultural College
ABAC 12, 2802 Moore Highway
Tifton, GA 31794-2601
(912) 386-3267

Idaho

Boise State University
College of Education
1910 University Drive
Boise, ID 83725
(208) 385-1754

University of Idaho
College of Education
Moscow, ID 83843
(208) 885-6205

Pennsylvania

Pennsylvania State University
Office of Sponsored Programs
2089 Boucke Building
University Park, PA 16802-7000
(814) 863-9440

Puerto Rico

InterAmerican University of Puerto Rico
San Germán Campus
P.O. Box 5100
San Germán, PR 00683-5100
(787) 264-1912

Texas

St. Edward's University
3001 South Congress Avenue
Austin, TX 78704-6489
(512) 488-8625

Texas A&M University–Kingsville
Division of Special Programs
Campus Box 181
Kingsville, TX 78363
(512) 593-2494

University of Texas Pan American
1201 W. University Drive
Edinburg, TX 78539-2999
(956) 381-2521

West Texas A&M University
2501 Fourth Avenue
P.O. Box 60731
Canyon, TX 79016-0003
(806) 651-5286

Chapter Eight
☙ Print and Nonprint Resources

Center for Research on Education, Diversity & Excellence (CREDE)
University of California
1156 High Street
Santa Cruz, CA 95064
(831) 459-3500
www.crede.ucsc.edu

The Center for Research on Education, Diversity & Excellence (CREDE) has a mission "to assist the nation's diverse students at risk of educational failure to achieve academic excellence." The center conducts research and publishes books, research reports, research briefs, and digests of information on issues of importance to the success of at-risk students, including migrant and bilingual education.

ERIC Clearinghouse on Languages and Linguistics
Center for Applied Linguistics
4646 40th Street NW
Washington, DC 20016-1859
(202) 362-0700
www.cal.org

The Clearinghouse on Languages and Linguistics provides services and materials for language educators. The Clearinghouse materials and services focus on English as a Second Language (ESL), bilingual education, intercultural communication, and cultural education.

ERIC Rural Education and Small Schools Clearinghouse
Appalachia Educational Laboratory
P.O. Box 1348
Charleston, WV 25325-1348
222.ael.org/eric

The ERIC Rural Education and Small Schools Clearinghouse maintains an extensive database of resources about migrant education. These include ERIC Digests, research articles, evaluations of migrant education programs, and other documents published by the U.S. Department of Education.

National Clearinghouse for Bilingual Education
George Washington University
Graduate School of Education and Human Development
Institute for Education Policy Studies
2121 K Street NW Suite 260
Washington, DC 20037
Contact: Dr. Minerva Gorena, Director
(800) 321-NCBE (6223)
(202) 467-0867 (within DC area)
http://www.ncbe.gwu.edu

The National Clearinghouse for Bilingual Education (NCBE) is funded by the U.S. Department of Education Office of Bilingual Education and Minority Languages Affairs (OBEMLA). NCBE collects, analyzes, and disseminates information about the effective education of linguistically and culturally diverse learners in the United States.

NCBE publishes *issue & brief,* a series of monographs that deal with topics related to their mission, as well as a weekly news bulletin, *Newsline.* The NCBE Web site also hosts online discussion groups on topics of interest to educators of linguistically and culturally diverse learners, the *Roundtable Forum.*

National Clearinghouse for ESL Literacy
Center for Applied Linguistics
4646 40th Street NW
Washington, DC 20016-1859
www.cal.org

This Clearinghouse, a special project of the Clearinghouse on Language and Linguistics, deals solely with research, materials, and services related to adult ESL literacy. Materials and services from the National Clearinghouse for ESL Literacy are, for the most part, provided to educators free of charge.

RESOURCES FOR TEACHERS AND ADMINISTRATORS OF MIGRANT EDUCATION PROGRAMS

Best S.E.L.F. *Best S.E.L.F.: Creating the Masterpiece.* Mount Vernon, WA: Elite Productions, 1999.

This video, available from Best S.E.L.F., 700 S. 2nd Street, Room 202, Mount Vernon, Washington 98273, (360) 336-9491, describes the Best S.E.L.F. program in the words of the children who participate in the program and the adults who work in it. The video shows children participating in recreation activities, hands-on experiential learning activities, and community service activities.

Best S.E.L.F. *Best S.E.L.F.: An Advocate Program of Excellence for Children. Replication Manual.* Mount Vernon, WA: Best S.E.L.F., 2001.

The *Best S.E.L.F. Replication Manual* provides guidelines for beginning and operating a community-based enrichment education program for children. It describes how to establish goals and develop a mission, how to build a community base of support and actively involve the community, how to raise funds, and how to recruit and train staff. The manual uses examples from the Skagit County Best S.E.L.F. program to illustrate each of these parts of developing such a program. The manual is available from Best S.E.L.F. at 700 S. 2nd Street, Room 202, Mount Vernon, Washington 98273, (360) 336-9491.

ESCORT (Eastern Stream Center on Resources and Training). *Help! They Don't Speak English Starter Kit for Primary Teachers. A Resource Guide for Educators of Limited English Proficient Migrant Students, Grades Pre-K-6.* 3d ed. Oneonta, NY: ESCORT, 1998.

This resource guide provides information to elementary teachers of migrant children who have limited proficiency in English. It includes cultural information; general and content-specific teaching strategies that integrate language development; assessment methods; ideas for involving language-minority parents; and resources for teachers.

Gonzales, M., D. Goldstein, E. Stief, L. Fiester, L. Weiner, and K. Waiters. *Even Start Projects Serving Migrant Families: Resource Guide.* 1998. Available from ERIC: ED424082.

This resource guide describes Migrant Education Even Start projects and how to establish and implement such a project. It includes appendices that list state Even Start and Migrant Education directors, sources of Migrant Education and Even Start technical assistance, sample forms, and text from legislation and regulations from the Federal Register.

Migrant Education Technology and Curriculum Resources. Available: http://lone-eagles.com/migrant.htm

Funded by the U.S. Department of Education's Office of Migrant Education, this recently constructed Web site offers links to information on Migrant Education Technology Projects, Federal and State Migrant Education resources, Spanish-language sites and search engines, and Spanish-language curriculum.

Play and Learn Books. Available from Working in Harmony, 380 #10 Road, Dexter, ME 04930 (207) 924-5560, alchemy@nconline.net

The *Play and Learn* books, developed by a migrant educator in Maine, have been distributed to all migrant families in Maine. They comprise kits of games and other materials for parents and children to work on together at home. Each of the kits includes a zipper pouch of all the materials necessary for the activities, including such tools as crayons, scissors, tangrams, game pieces, calculators, and so on. There are three kits in the series, one for preschoolers, *Little PAL;* one for elementary students, *Family PAL;* and *Math PAL,* a comprehensive tool kit for basic math, algebra, geometry, and trigonometry for middle and high school students. The *Little PAL* and *Family PAL* kits are also available in Spanish.

Rios, O., M. Rivera, and M. Solis, eds. ***GEMS: Graduation Enhancement for Migrant Students.*** 1977. (ERIC Document Reproduction Service No. 491640)

This handbook was developed to assist educators in understanding the unique needs of migrant students and to offer suggestions for addressing those issues to support migrant students in graduation from high school. The handbook addresses counseling and guidance services, planning for postsecondary education and the workplace, Texas graduation requirements, credit options available to migrant students, student leadership programs, alternatives for late entry and early withdrawal, English-language acquisition, student personal development, and recovery programs. The handbook is also available from the STAR Center, Intercultural Development Research Association, 5835 Callaghan Road, Suite 350, San Antonio, Texas 78228-1190, and by phone at (210) 684-8180, by fax at (210) 684-5389, or by e-mail at idra@idra.org.

Siler, A., S. Stolzberg, A. von Glatz, and W. Strang. ***Meeting the Needs of Migrant Students in Schoolwide Programs. Technical Report of the Congressionally Mandated Study of Migrant Student Participation in Schoolwide Program.*** Washington, D.C.: U.S. Department of Education Planning and Evaluation Service, 1999.

This report provides information about how migrant students are served in Title I schoolwide programs. It includes case studies of twenty-five schoolwide programs that serve migrant students. The report is available from the U.S. Department of Education Office of Migrant Education.

Western Stream Migrant Education Program Coordination Center. ***Steppin' On Up: A Post-Secondary Guide for Migrant Students—Tomando accion: Una guia para los estudiantes migrantes sobre que hacer despues de la escuela secondaria.*** 1996. (ERIC Document Reproduction Service No. ED 398000)

This guide, in English and Spanish, provides information for migrant high school students about postsecondary education. It includes information on careers, how to plan during high school for postsecondary education, where and how to apply for financial aid, and CAMP (the College Assistance Migrant Program).

INFORMATION ON MIGRANT HEALTH ISSUES

National Center for Farmworker Health. ***Resource Center Catalog.*** Austin, TX: National Center for Farmworker Health, 2001. Available: http://www.ncfh.org

This online catalog provides a wide variety of resources about migrant health, including artwork, videos, patient education materials, health care provider resources, and research materials. Several of the sets of material available through the catalog are aimed at children, including a video, *The Playing Field,* about the dangers of pesticide exposure, and health curriculum kits for children in the primary and intermediate grades.

INFORMATION ABOUT SCHOLARSHIPS
FOR MIGRANT STUDENTS

Daimler Chrysler. ***On the Road to Higher Education: Guide to Hispanic***

Financial Aid Opportunities. Highland Park, MI: DaimlerChrysler, 2000.

The Daimler Chrysler Corporation publishes an annual listing of scholarships available for Hispanic students. Besides the list of scholarships, the guide includes suggestions for application and a list of Hispanic-serving colleges and universities. These colleges and universities have a minimum enrollment of 25 percent Hispanic students. The free publication is available by writing to Daimler Chrysler Guide to Hispanic Financial Aid Oppportunities, P.O. Box 3189, Highland Park, MI 48203, or telephone (800) 521-0953. The financial aid information is also available on line at www.HispanicScholarship.com

PathtoScholarships.com
P.O. Box 536
Oakland, FL 34760
(407) 877-9630

This Web site provides information about accessing postsecondary education. It includes information for ordering a publication that describes sources of financial aid for migrant students.

MEDIA PRESENTATIONS ABOUT MIGRANT LIFESTYLE AND EDUCATION

National Association of State Directors of Migrant Education (NASDME). *Harvesting Dreams, Launching Futures: Commemorating Thirty-five Years of Migrant Education.* Helena, MT: National Association of State Directors of Migrant Education, 2001.

This multimedia presentation is available on CD ROM from the Montana Migrant Education Program, P.O. Box 202501, Helena, MT 59620-2501, (406) 444-2509. The presentation includes nearly 300 photographs of the migrant experience, including work, housing and education, as well as poetry written by migrant students.

Tejada-Flores, R., and R. Telles. *The Fight in the Fields: César Chavez and the Farmworkers' Struggle.* ITVS, 2001.

This film about the life of César Chavez and the history of the United Farmworkers and their struggle has been aired by PBS. Information about the airing of the film is available at www.pbs.org/itvs/fightfields/

LITERATURE FOR CHILDREN AND YOUNG ADULTS ABOUT MIGRANT LIFESTYLE AND EDUCATION

Ada, A. F. *Gathering the Sun: An Alphabet in Spanish and English.* New York: Lothrop, Lee & Shepard, 1994.

This alphabet book of poems that describe life in the fields is written in Spanish and translated into English. The illustrator, Simón Silva, himself grew up in a migrant family and brings a special understanding of migrant life that is evident in the book's illustrations.

Atkins, S. B. *Voices from the Fields: Children of Migrant Farmworkers Tell Their Stories.* Boston: Little, Brown and Company, 1993.

This book tells the stories of migrant children in their own words. The children's stories, in Spanish and English, poetry and prose, are accompanied by photographs that provide additional context.

Brimmer, L. D. *A Migrant Family.* Minneapolis: Lerner, 1992.

This book describes the life of a migrant family as they travel to work in the fields in language that children can understand.

Buirski, N. *Earth Angels.* San Francisco: Pomegranate Art Books, 1994.

Migrant life is shown in this book through a series of poignant photographs that depict the working and living conditions faced by migrant farmworker families.

Bunting, E. *A Day's Work.* New York: Clarion Books, 1994.

This picture book, illustrated by Ronald Himler, tells the story of a young Mexican American boy who translates for his grandfather, who does not speak English. The boy helps his grandfather find a job and in the process learns an important life lesson from his grandfather. It is a story about a migrant child taking responsibility beyond his years.

Hoyt-Goldsmith, D. *Migrant Worker: A Boy from the Rio Grande Valley.* New York: Holiday House, 1996.

This book tells the story of Ricky, an eleven-year-old migrant worker, who travels from his home in Texas. Ricky and his family work ten or more hours a day picking fruit and vegetables and packing the produce for the market. The book also includes a profile of César Chavez.

Jiménez, F. ***The Circuit: Stories from the Life of a Migrant Child.*** Albu-querque, NM: University of New Mexico Press, 1997.

The author, now a professor at Santa Clara University, draws on his own experience of growing up in a migrant farmworker family and tells sto-ries about traveling and picking fruit in California. The book describes the travels of one family from site to site, and from school to school, from the perspective of a young boy. It includes poignant descriptions of the substandard housing conditions and health care the family faced, the feelings of this child as he repeatedly left schools and friends, the poverty of the family, and the language, cultural, and educational dis-continuity they faced.

Jiménez, F. ***La Mariposa.*** Boston: Houghton Mifflin Company, 1998.

The author took one chapter of his book, *The Circuit,* and republished it as a picture book. In it, he describes his own struggle to understand the language and the culture of the school. The book includes a glossary of the Spanish words included in the English version of the text. Simón Silva's beautiful illustrations show his understanding of the life of mi-grant children; he himself grew up in a migrant farmworker family. A Spanish edition of this text is also available.

Williams, S. A. ***Working Cotton.*** San Diego, CA: Voyager Books, 1992.

Beautifully illustrated by Carole Byard, this book chronicles a day in the life of a migrant family who pick cotton. Beginning on a bus ride to the fields before dawn, and ending at sunset waiting for the bus to take the family home, the story is told from the perspective of a child who must work in the fields with her parents.

MIGRANT EDUCATION TECHNOLOGY GRANT PROJECTS

Anchor School
University of North Carolina at Greensboro
http://www.anchorschool.org
(910) 334-4667
Contact: Jean Williams

Anchor School provides support for students and families migrating from Florida up the eastern seaboard.

★ESTRELLA
Illinois Migrant Council
http://www.estrella.org
(312) 633-1522
Contact: Brenda Pessin

★ESTRELLA uses laptop computers and cyber mentors to keep students on track toward high school graduation.

InTIME
Oregon Department of Education
http://www.intime.k12.or.us
(503) 391-9480
Contact: David Rosalez

InTIME serves migrant students in Oregon through public television, electronic assessment, and technology integrated learning.

KMTP
Ohio Valley Education Cooperative
http://migrant.org
(502) 222-0748
Contact: Michael Abell

KMTP uses technology to support the K-12 migrant students and families in Kentucky.

Project MECHA
Barry University
http://mecha.barry.edu
(305) 899-3031
Contact: Dr. Janie Greenleaf

Project MECHA supports migrant students with Web TV.

⚡ Index